BEYOND BLOGGING
The Secrets to Blogging Success!

Nathan Hangen &
Mike Cliffe Jones

Copyright © 2009 Beyond Blogging Corp.

Published by Beyond Blogging Corp, Tampa, FL.

No part of this publication may be reproduced, stored in a retrieval system, or transmitted in any form or by any means, electronic, mechanical, photocopying, recording, scanning, or otherwise, except as permitted under section 107 or 108 of the 1976 United States Copyright Act, without either the prior written permission of the Publisher. Requests to the Publisher for permission should be addressed to the Beyond Blogging Corp., 6721 Saint Julian Way, Fayetteville, NC, 28314 or online at http://beyond-blogging.net.

Limite of Liability/Disclaimer of Warranty: While the publisher and author have used their best efforts in preparing this book, they make no representations or warranties with respect to the accuracy or completeness of the contents of this book and specifically disclaim any implied warranties of merchantability or fitness for a particular purpose. No warranty may be created or extended by sales representitives or written sales materials. The advice and strategies contained herein may not be suitable for your situation. You should consult with a professional where appropriate. Neither the publisher nor author shall be liable for any loss of profit or any other commercial damages, including but not limited to special, incidental, consequential, or other damages.

For general information on our other products and services, or for technical support, please visit our website at http://beyond-blogging.net.

ISBN: 145-0505-392

Printed in the United States of America

10 9 8 7 6 5 4 3 2 1

table of contents

Foreword 9
Featured Bloggers 18
    How to Crush It 21
    Challenging Authority Since 1978 37
    The Original Geek 53
    A Master of Networking 65
    The Brazen Blogger 81
    Straight Shooting Six Figure Blogger 93
Case Studies 106
    Self Styled Dot Com Mogul 109
    The Internet's Brad Pitt 121
    The Zen Marketer's Group 129
    The Young One 139
    Career Renegade 149
    The Problogge Himself 159
    Video Star 169
    The Original Personal Development Blogger 181
    The Real Man behind the Curtain 189
The Six Figure Blogging Blueprint 198

Foreword

We want to be able to take trips, spoil our wife and children, and slow down and enjoy life. We'll show you how to do that

Foreword

Nathan Hangen

Wow, what a crazy year! In 2009 alone, I spent 8 months in Afghanistan working with the Department of State and US Army, 4 months training for the Augusta Half Ironman in September, and countless hours plotting and planning my future business ventures. While I was deployed, I used my free time to dive into the depths of Internet Marketing, blogging, and serial entrepreneurship in the hope that I could find a way to transition out of the Army without having to get a job. Thanks to a lot of hard work, my eyes, as Gary Vaynerchuk says "bleeding at the computer," and my determination to follow my passion, I think I might have finally found that way.

The truth is, I started blogging because I felt like I had to get it out. The quote "don't die with your music still inside of you" rang true for me as I decided to start blogging my interests with the only goal being to satisfy the inner muse and release my "music" to the world. Eventually, I was inspired by the people we'll feature in this book, and my blogging took on a life of its own. Soon after that, I started connecting with other bloggers and realized that I wasn't the only one with this quest. Furthermore, I was actually developing a readership, something I never expected to happen.

Eventually, I created over a dozen various blogs on some of my favorite topics, many of which now make me money or help me build my personal brand, which we will talk about in the bulk of this book.

Although blogging is a lifestyle effort of personal branding and entrepreneurial spirit, it also feeds the soul. Since I started releasing my thoughts to the world, I found that I've never been happier. Sure, there are times when I'm nervous as hell after I hit the publish button, but I wouldn't trade that feeling away for the world. I've always believed that being nervous shows that you care, and as long as I get nervous I'll still feel like I have life left.

As for the way in which blogging can fuel your own business, I don't believe that there is another vehicle that is as powerful as blogging is for doing so. Properly done, blogging can help you create an authority presence in the niche of your choosing. When you combine that with passion, you get a recipe for making money doing what you love.

I don't care if you love telescopes, blue suede shoes, or custom picture frames, there is a niche out there waiting for you to take charge. If you truly follow your passion, I believe that you can make any number of things, all positive, happen for you. You'll have to work hard, and yes you might have to make sacrifices, but if you are doing what you love, then what more can you ask for?

Foreword

Blogging can help you get that book deal you've always wanted, and in this book we will show you how it can be done. You can create an empire of big or small money making websites so that you can help people and make money doing what you love. Turn it all on auto-pilot and you've figured out how to make a living while spending more time having fun. That's really the dream isn't it? Most of us want to find a way to make money without having to sacrifice personal or family time. We want to be able to take trips, spoil our wife and children, and slow down and enjoy life. We'll show you how to do that.

If taking it easy isn't your thing, then we'll show you how to really kick your business into overdrive so you can create wealth beyond your wildest dreams. You can create an empire if you have the passion and desire to do so. The important thing is to follow your dreams and enrich the lives of others. Once you figure out how to tap into that well of excellence, there will be no one that can hold you back.

Gatekeepers beware, we're on the warpath and we aren't taking any prisoners.

I hope you enjoy this book as much as Mike and I enjoyed creating it. We wish you nothing but success, may your dreams be bright and your life even brighter

Nathan Hangen, North Carolina, USA.

http://NathanHangen.com

twitter.com/nhangen

Bloggers are the new media superstars, wielding the power of enormous audiences that would make old time newspaper moguls green with envy

Foreword

Mike Cliffe-Jones

I had the most conventional of careers until 2008. I worked for 18 years for very large corporations, working my way up their ladders to become a successful senior manager. Then I quit the rat race (or thought I did) by moving to a small Atlantic Island and starting a bricks and mortar business. Inevitably, with lots of hard work, it became a big business, and before I knew it I was back in the 9-5 routine.

I've been a writer all my life, and had always dreamed of being published. That dream came true for me in 2008 when my book, **Living in Lanzarote** hit the shops.

The joy of being paid for my words convinced me that I could create the career I'd always wanted from writing, and I once again left security and stability behind to start a new life at the keyboard.

I now run a stable of blogs which earn me a good living, I'm working on two new books, and I'm loving every minute of my new lifestyle.

The success I have enjoyed as a blogger, in a relatively short time, is largely thanks to the help and support I've enjoyed from some of the bloggers featured in this book.

Beyond Blogging is the book that can help you to do the same. Nathan and I dissect the secrets of the world's greatest bloggers and share with you a roadmap that distils their stories into easy to follow steps.

As long as you can write, you can achieve an income on-line, and if you're really talented, and prepared to put in some serious hard work, you can join the ranks of the new elite.

Bloggers are the new media superstars, wielding the power of enormous audiences that would make old time newspaper moguls green with envy.

Millions follow their words and thoughts, hundreds of thousands interact with them via comments, and tens of thousands receive their email newsletters. And they can do all this from a single computer in their own homes. Because of the size of their readerships, one post promoting a product, or one book with their names on it can generate vast revenues in the time it takes to make a post live.

I'm delighted and proud that we've been able to work with the very top names in the industry for this book. We set out to get an all-star cast for **Beyond Blogging**, and we succeeded!

I'm sure we've done justice to them, and I'm certain this book will help you to achieve whatever you want in the world of blogging, and beyond.

Foreword

Finally, I'd like to dedicate this book to all the people in the world who want to write, in the hope that we may help you start your own journey as a writer.

Mike Cliffe-Jones, Lanzarote, Canary Islands

http://MikesLife.org

twitter.com/mikecj

Featured Bloggers

How to Crush It

Hanging out with your audience is where you really make your money. Having great content isn't going to help you if you can't convince your readers to come back

Gary Vaynerchuk

Gary Vaynerchuk is a man that is on fire. He's dominating both new and old media alike and seems to be still building momentum for even bigger things to come. He's just launched his first of 10 books, a high profile new media consulting agency, and has been featured on *Conan O'Brien, The Ellen show, Mad Money, Nightline,* and nearly a dozen other TV spots. He's been called the "Brian Tracy of new media," "the wine guy," and everything in between.

There is no question that his audience will continue to grow; the only question that remains is just how big it can get.

For Gary, it all began when his father Sasha brought the family from Belarus to the United States in 1978. Gary was 3 at the time, but remembers growing up and watching his father build a business the old fashioned way…through hard work and dedication. At the time, the small liquor store, called *Shopper's Discount Liquors*, looked nothing like the *Wine Library* it would become, but it is obvious that the entrepreneurial roots are strong in the Vaynerchuk family.

It's All about Hustle

When Gary was young, he remembers opening up lemonade stands throughout his neighborhood. He'd get one started and then recruit his friends to run them so that he could open others. From lemonade franchises, Gary moved to baseball cards, where he used local card shows and online chat rooms to build an empire selling, what he says, were not always the most sought after cards. In fact, Gary mentioned that there was a time when he borrowed $1,000 from his father to buy baseball cards to sell at an upcoming baseball card show.

Later, when he opened the several hundred packs of baseball cards, his heart sank when he realized that his $1,000 in cash was worth only about $200 in baseball card currency. Undeterred, Gary still found a way to unload the cards for a profit, thanks to his strategy of scouting the competition and pricing just below them.

Two years later, when he was 18, Gary began to work for his father at the liquor store, doing everything from stocking, to cleaning the floors. Although the work was less glamorous then making a killing selling baseball cards, Gary made use of the experience by studying his ass off and learning as much about wine as he could. Even during college, he came home on the weekends to work at the store and build his chops in the wine world.

Finally, in 1997, Gary convinced his father to launch <u>WineLibrary.com</u>, at which point everything else is history. Gary helped the store improve revenue from 2 million per year to over 10 million per year, and doubled it again 2 years later.

His experience selling baseball cards helped him learn the basics of building a business, while his understanding of the wine world helped him cash in on a previously undersold niche. It wasn't until 2006 that Gary launched **Wine Library TV**, which is where he started an assault on modern marketing, old media, and tired personal branding tactics.

The inspiring part about Gary's story is not that he turned a wine business around, but that he's learned how to dominate the game on all fronts. Obviously, Gary has had a passion for business throughout his entire life, but he's proven that he can do it with any business and at any time.

If you haven't watched Gary do his thing on <u>GaryVaynerchuk.com</u> or <u>Wine Library TV</u>, then you're missing out on a fireball of energy and passion. When talking to him, you get a sense of how much he loves what he does, but when he told me that the main reason he launched **Wine Library TV** was to connect with people, I realized how important it is to let people, not money, drive your business.

Love What You Do

His strategy is clear, but it takes a special type of person to pull it off. It starts with being absolutely in love with what you are doing. Gary told us that if you are in business for anything other than doing what you love, then you are setting yourself up for failure. He's said it many times, but the reason he launched *Wine Library TV* was that he wanted to go from being 99.99% happy to 100% happy…that's how important it was to him.

It doesn't just stop there though; you've got to cash in on that passion by using solid business tactics and getting to the heart of where the community lives. According to Gary, most people don't want to do the hard work of building networks and creating communities. When we asked Gary how he built his audience at *Wine Library*, he said he spent a majority of his time in chat rooms, blog comment sections, and in message boards. He built his audience by recruiting one fan at a time. When he only had 7 fans, he loved those 7 fans to death. Eventually, those 7 brought in 25, which turned into 100, etc.

Gary makes use of every medium, both new and old, to attract and interact with his fans. Although you can usually find him on morning and late night talk shows, Gary also makes heavy use of Facebook fan pages, USTREAM, and Twitter. Gary is one of the early pioneers of using USTREAM as a medium to connect with an audience, and many others have piggybacked on his success there. It makes sense though, that if you have an audience eager to interact with you, that creating your own interactive platform, makes you larger than life to those fans. You won't find many musicians or Hollywood stars doing things like that, which is why Gary has managed to become a new sort of star, or as he calls it, a "triple Z List celebrity."

To keep the community around, Gary said you need to not only have great content, but you need to publish it on a consistent basis. *Wine Library TV* published a new episode every single day, rain or shine. At first glance you might wonder how you can talk about wine every single day for 30-60 minutes, especially with the same energy and passion as you did on the first. But somehow, Gary was able to pull it off. He said that regardless of whether or not he had 1 fan, or 100, he would do each show as if he was talking to millions. He never doubted his potential and refused to take the easy road, which should be an example to all of us that are looking for an excuse to quit when times get tough.

Finally, Gary did a fantastic job of creating a brand around his show. He had the Jets spit bucket, was talking about He-Man and Thundercats, and compared wine to dirt, leather, and candy. At the time, wine critics were down on Gary because he took a cultured industry and brought it down to the level of the everyday man, but that's been Gary's shtick all along. He was tired of wine snobs using tired language to talk about wine, thinking that it scared people away. He realized that if he simply changed the culture of wine, he'd attract an untapped audience to not only appreciate wine, but to buy it.

Later, Gary created branded versions of apparel, such as his *Wine Library* and Gary V wristbands that created a culture around his daily show. Gary became a rockstar in the industry because he made it cool to like wine and even more importantly, made it cool to join the Vayner Nation.

What I really like about Gary's model, is that he used the success of his wine show to launch his own website, GaryVaynerchuk.com, so that he could expand his focus to more than just wine. Clearly, Gary understands business, so it only made sense to create a platform to educate and inspire others to create their own businesses. Although his posting there has slowed down significantly, going through the early posts will give you an idea of how close he lives to the cutting edge of business and social media trends.

Clearly, Gary wasn't going to stop there though, as he leveraged his rabid audience into speaking gigs across the nation. The topics vary from keynote to keynote, but more often than not, the main points that Gary likes to drive home are:

- Thanks to new media, all bets are off. Anyone can start a business and build their own platform without relying on the gatekeepers of the old media.

- If you aren't doing what you love, you are wrong. There is no excuse not to create a business around your passion.
- There are fans in every niche, simply recruit them and evangelize.

Although Gary makes it all look easy, the truth is that he hustles more than anyone I've ever seen. In fact, when we set out to interview him, we were offered times anywhere from 6AM to midnight, proof that Gary really is "Crushing It" every single night.

Using Gary's Strategy to Your Advantage

We know how Gary did it, but let's take a step back to talk about how you can implement Gary's strategy and create a successful blogging business on your own. To begin, it's clear that you need to take time to understand what really drives you…what you are passionate about. Although it might seem like Gary's passion is wine, the truth is that wine was just the vehicle for his passion of building businesses. Gary is proof that you can create a business around a variety of topics, so don't feel like you are limiting yourself by picking one topic. That's just the place where you need to start.

Once you've found that reason to wake up in the morning, that topic that really drives you, then you need to make sure that you are the expert. Being the most passionate simply isn't good enough; you need to be an expert in your field. Again, this is where many people simply don't want to do the hard work, but you can't skip this step if you want to be successful. Read books, study the experts in your field, and keep learning. You don't have to wait until you are the expert, but you should definitely have a base of knowledge before you start blogging.

From there, you need to create great content, consistently. Although Gary's medium is video, there's no reason the same tactics can't work for a typical text blog or a podcast. Gary's suggestion was that you find which medium you feel most comfortable using and then become a master at that medium. Although it never hurts to offer a variety of media on your blog, being consistent is the key.

Although Gary created a new show on **Wine Library TV** every single day, there's no reason why you can't stick to 3-5 times per week instead. However, try to create a schedule and stick to it. That way, your audience knows when to tune in for new content and doesn't get upset at an erratic schedule. As most bloggers will tell you, deviating from your published schedule will usually result in backlash of some sort. So, tell your readers/viewers what to expect, and then make sure you stand by your word.

The interesting thing about Gary's medium, is that he actually doesn't use it to directly monetize *Wine Library*. It is also interesting to note that they only carry a limited quantity of the wines he features on the show. He says his goal is to get more people to enjoy wine, and although that's certainly part of the formula, the wines on the show sell out almost instantly. That's the power of building an audience eager for content. He's actually selling wine without even asking for the sale…now that's power.

Power to the People

Speaking of an audience, according to Gary, hanging out with your audience is where you really make your money. Having great content isn't going to help you if you can't convince your readers to come back. For many, this is one of the greatest challenges to overcome. There are millions of blogs, thousands of bloggers, and massive amounts of audio and video content online already, so your task is to stand out among that crowd.

The most effective way to do this is to get people to like you, which is why Gary spent most of his time engaging with his community.

If you are new to social media, Gary recommends that you spend a few months immersing yourself in the processes and systems that make social media work. However, if you don't want to learn it, then you either need to find someone to do it for you, or spend a lot of money on marketing, which is far less effective in terms of converting effort into dollars.

If you've got the chops to get out and talk with people, then you should be creating a presence on Facebook, Twitter, YouTube, USTREAM , and in as many blog comment sections as you can afford to. Use Google blog search to find other blogs on your topic and then go out and recruit those readers. Treat every comment on your blog like it's the most important comment you've ever received, and work hard to convert your loyal fans into devotees.

Gary mentioned that for 6-9 months he wasn't receiving any more than 5-6 comments per episode, and this was after creating 30 minutes of content every single day!

Over time though, the effort will pay off, but you can't give up before it does. When we asked Gary if he had a backup plan, he said it never occurred to him that he would fail at this, he was in 100%. That doesn't mean you can't tweak your message along the way, but people that are constantly looking for a reason to quit usually end up using failure as an excuse rather than as a lesson learned.

Once you have your audience in place, the next step is simply a matter of always looking to expand your game. For Gary, it was launching GaryVaynerchuk.com and speaking at keynotes. For you, it could mean an additional platform in another niche, or working with JV partners to expand your current platform. Networking with the other stars in your niche is just as important as networking with the audience. Through these conversations, you can work your way into speaking gigs, which is how Gary was able to snag his book deal.

It was after he spoke at a keynote that Gary was approached for the mega book deal with Harper Studio, but if that's the avenue that you are looking to approach, then consider having a book proposal written and ready to send out to publishers and book agents. Always be ready for the next step of the adventure, and always think monetization.

Gary talks of monetization as if it comes naturally, but most of us struggle to market ourselves, either due to fear or low self-confidence. Don't get in the way of your success…if you've got a rockstar system or a lifetime of experience, then find a way to market that ability as a consultant or a speaker. If that's not your style, then sell advertising, not by waiting for it to come, but by actively seeking out advertisers on your own.

Last, but certainly not least, you've got to hustle. If you have a job that keeps you busy during the day, then take advantage of the evening hours, when your family is in bed, to build your business. Gary recommends that you spend 75% of your time marketing and networking, and the other 25% creating great content. Don't expect results overnight, it can take months to gain traction, but if you want to "Crush It", then you've got to own the night.

Gary told us that all this "4 Hour Workweek" stuff is garbage. He said that if you really love what you do, then you won't have time for TV or watching movies and playing video games. You'll be "bleeding out of your eyes" at the computer every single night. Even now, Gary works tirelessly, always looking to get an edge on his competition and always looking to spend more time with his audience. Anytime you see his name pop up on a blog, you'll be sure to see a response from him at some point. Gary acknowledged that being everywhere isn't easy, but he relies on his instinct and his team to help guide his focus, which as of now, is to be the best Gary V he can be.

The same should hold true for you. Setting goals is important, but Gary says that it's more important to be true to your DNA. This means that you need to do whatever you feel called to do, and do it with as much passion and energy as you can muster. If you stay authentic and real, your audience will respond and love you for it. If you act like someone else, you're going to have a much harder time keeping that facade on and eventually, someone will call you out for it. I think Gary puts it best when he says, "you can't chase someone else's dream, or else you'll be chasing it forever." If you stick to what you believe in, and do it every single day with vigor, you'll eventually make the right connections to take your business to the next level.

How to Crush It

Looking back, it's amazing to think that Gary Vaynerchuk only popped on the radar a few years ago. He's literally been all over the map, dominating every aspect of the game. The thing is, there's only one Gary Vaynerchuk, so although it is great to model his success and vision, remember that you have to follow your own path to be successful. However, you would be selling yourself short if you didn't grab a copy of Gary's book, **Crush It**, and watch how he brings the screen to life at **Wine Library TV**. With **Wine Library** doing business in the millions, his 10 book deal bringing him 7 figures, and Vayner Media taking off, Gary has certainly learned how to cash in on his passion. There is no reason that the rest of us can't follow his advice and do the same.

Challenging Authority
Since 1978

One good guest post for an A-list blog has more impact than anything I've written for CNN, Business Week, or the New York Times thus far.

Challenging Authority Since 1978

Chris Guillebeau

Perhaps no blogger's rise to success has been as quick and as impactful as that of Art of Non-Conformity blogger, Chris Guillebeau. Chris' project, the <u>Art of Non-Conformity</u> (**AONC**), has earned the praise and support of dozens of old media outlets, hundreds of A-List bloggers, and thousands of eyeballs across the world. Chris' is a remarkable story for other reasons too, as his mission is both inspiring and an exciting example of how many traditional boundaries can be broken if one has a sufficient plan and the dedication to pull it off.

He fashions himself as a world dominator, meaning that he's determined to prove that people don't have to live life like they are told to. To him, this means taking on traditional gatekeepers and either bypassing them by creating a new slice of the pie, or knocking them down by creating a small army to help you take the world by storm.

Although many people know Chris as the guy that travels to countries all over the world (sometimes in the same week), he's also a vegetarian, marathon runner, and dedicated husband. Even though Chris doesn't often talk about his wife Jolie, he says both her advice and her support are crucial to his success.

Chris spent two years in Asia as a child, but says he didn't start traveling until 2006, when he began a 4 year stint working for a medical charity in West Africa. It was during this time that, in his words, he gave "keynote speeches to presidents, hung out with warlords, and learned far more in those four years than anything I learned in college."

From there, Chris toyed around with several online business models, including selling imported Jamaican coffee on eBay, AdSense arbitrage, and SEO services. Although he was fairly successful using these strategies, you get the feeling in talking to him that he wanted more from his life than the ability to just pay the bills. Yes, his primary motivation in creating an online business was, as he put it, to "avoid having to work for the man," but he still felt like there was more to his story.

As of September of 2006, Chris had already decided he wanted to visit every country in the world, but until now he hadn't created an action plan. Feeling compelled to make a change, Chris returned to the United States, where he attended the University of Washington, but more importantly, created a launching pad for his world travels. With amazing tenacity, Chris used his free time between quarters and on the weekends to plan his trips across the globe, and consistently visited over 20 countries per year.

It was during this time, as he started keeping journals of his travels, that he knew he might be on to something. So he began to turn his journal entries into essays online, and thus ***The Art of Non-Conformity Project*** was born. What began as an initial concept, and later a beta project with a select handful of readers, eventually grew into a core readership of over 15,000, an income approaching six figures, and a lifestyle that, as of October 2009, helped him set foot on 119 out of the 197 countries in the world.

From there, Chris' story has been picked up by major media outlets, such as the *New York Times*, the *Washington Times*, and MSNBC. He's inked a book deal with Perigee, writes for the *Oregonian*, among others, and his manifestos have been downloaded over 100,000 times from countries all over the world. Let's just say that Chris' star is bright, but it appears to be growing even brighter.

Although it might seem as if Chris found instant success online, we'd be doing his story an injustice if we gave you only the beginning and end, as it is the middle portion that is perhaps the most important, and the most beneficial to you.

Any time a blogger reaches the level of success it might look like it was easy, but the truth is that it is far from easy to duplicate this kind of success. This isn't to say that it cannot be done, but you can't do it without a plan. Fortunately for us, Chris has shared this blueprint, so let's get started.

While other bloggers might come up with a fancy name or title for their blog, Chris thought it would be important to use his own name as the brand, rather than the title of his project. This allows him to remain above the project, and promote his work as a publisher. It also allows him to create a presence that doesn't rely on the *AONC Project*, meaning that now that his brand is successful, he can take his game to the next level, regardless of the state of *AONC*.

This point is important, because if you want to alter your path or change your brand at any time during the growth process, you will face difficulty unless your name is brand independent. It's not that it cannot be done, but it is certainly something to consider in the early planning phases of your project.

When I asked Chris about what it takes to become successful as a blogger, he had good news for all of us. Even if you are failing now, Chris believes that anyone can make a living as a blogger as long as they can successfully answer a few important questions:

What is your story?

Do you have a strong enough why?

Can you combine what you love with what your audience loves?

Although Chris was able to gain a sizable readership in around six month's time, he already had a great story to tell, which helped him significantly. He estimates that for most people, it should take about a year to build a business online, which is still an encouraging number. The problem is that far too many quit before they've put in the effort

Challenging Authority Since 1978

required to make it happen. Although you might feel compelled to do the same, if you apply even a quarter of Chris' strategy, then I guarantee you'll see enough progress to give you the motivation to continue.

Let's start with your story. Chris believes that all of us have a compelling story buried within, but in order to make it attractive to our readers, we must frame it in a manner that strikes a chord with others. For example, Chris' story probably wouldn't have the same effect if he blogged about his travels from an elitist perspective. The part of Chris' story that compels people to follow along is that he makes it easy for anyone to do the same by sharing his knowledge via his weekly essays.

Had Chris' blog been just a travel blog and not an example of knocking down gatekeepers and creating your own path of world domination, he wouldn't stand out among the thousands of already existing travel blogs. It is the way that he ties in his entrepreneurial experience with his remarkable goal of visiting every country in the world that ensures people are inspired by him. He tells you not only what he does, but how you can do the same.

This brings us to the question of asking yourself how your readers can benefit from reading your blog. Chris says that if you don't spend enough time answering the "what's in it for me?" question, then you'll have a very difficult time gaining any traction. If you're doing all the right things but find that you just can't get your readers to hang around, then this might be your issue.

The way that Chris answered it was twofold:

1. By coming to his blog, his readers can live vicariously through his adventures or they can learn how to do the same by reading his book, essays, and manifestos.
2. Readers can take it a step further by joining his "small army," which is a cleverly crafted way of saying they can join his tribe, where they'll receive the support of a community and the benefit of feeling like they are part of the experiment.

Although the first answer is probably the most useful, the truth is that emotion is the primary driver for many human behaviors. People generally show up to Chris' site hoping to learn something about travel hacking or life hacking, but the reason they stick around is because they feel drawn to the atmosphere of the community. It is in this sense that Chris functions as a tribe leader, possibly more so than any of the other bloggers in this book.

The third question is perhaps the most important, and rightly so, as not understanding the needs of an audience can be any bloggers downfall. Whether you are a seasoned pro-blogger or a novice, forgetting about the needs of your audience can and will put you out of business.

Challenging Authority Since 1978

To answer the third question, it might help to make a list of what you love to do. Use a mind-mapping tool if it helps, but try to list everything that you do on a daily basis, love talking about, and spend most of your time thinking about. From there, take a look at the Amazon best seller list and try to get an idea of what kind of questions people have and topics that people are reading about. Do a Google blog search on your favorite topics and read some of the most popular blogs in those niches. Look through the posts and the comments and you'll start to see recurring themes. From there, you'll have a good idea of what people want. The next step then is to find a way that you can do it better or do it differently. This might mean going deeper into the niche or spreading out in order to combine some of your favorite topics.

Although Chris' niche might seem brilliantly obvious to you, don't think that Chris figured it out overnight. He created his **AONC** concept over the course of many months and took the time to plan his approach before he implemented it.

For those of you that think that Chris just happens to have what it takes or that being able to start your own tribe is as easy as saying you are open for business, don't be fooled. There are a lot of things that go on behind the scenes in order to allow this to happen, which is what we'll talk about next.

Design

The starting point for the *AONC* experience, and Chris will agree, is the first impression his site makes when they arrive on the site. Although many bootsrappers will tell you that getting started, regardless of practicality, usefulness, or attractiveness of the design is the most important step in opening up shop, the truth is that you only have around 3 seconds to make a first impression with a new reader. If your design detracts from your site in any way, then that reader is probably lost for good.

This is why Chris took on the search for a design and branding professional that understood his game (in this instance it was the fabulous designer Reese Spykerman, whom he met in Malaysia). This is also why he hired a professional photographer for the photos on his 1st generation website. Chris' savvy understanding of design impact and branding is one that probably cut months off of his growth curve.

If you visit his website now, you'll notice that the design has been improved a 2nd time. I believe this to be an example of how a blogger has never finished evolving and should always be looking to the next level.

Challenging Authority Since 1978

Content

Aside from the design, you can tell that Chris spends a great deal of time crafting his brand. Everything from his post titles, the quality of his writing, and the published editorial schedule do their part to tell the reader that this blog is for real. His essays are often over 1,000 words long and you can tell immediately upon visiting his site that he is not doing this "just for fun."

Sure, we've heard the "content is king" line no less than a thousand times, but most simply give lip service to the idea. Chris, on the other hand, believes his content to be the lifeline of his business, which is why he busts his ass to make sure he delivers each post on time and with consistent quality. If you take a look at his average post, you'll find that it is a case study for effective writing. He chunks his content to make it scanable by effectively using headings, subheadings, and bullets. It might not be noticeable to the unknowing reader, but it certainly impacts the user experience.

Creating Viral Content

Where many marketers might try to nickel and dime their audience until they either buy or go away, Chris strongly believes that it is more important to create a platform to spread your message than a store in which to sell it. Although he does offer a list of various products on his website, he has an anti-marketing strategy, which is evident in the number of free products he gives away.

One could argue that he should have charged for his most recent manifesto, 279 Days to Overnight Success, but the truth is that when he gave it away for free, without so much as an email required, he was able to gain far more reach than he could through blogging alone.

Major A-Listers, such as Seth Godin, spread his message for him and soon his popularity skyrocketed once more. For most people, it's tough to do that even with free content, but because Chris treated the release as a major launch, actively recruiting other bloggers (affiliates) and creating an email campaign long before the release date, he was able to blow up virtually overnight... again. True testament to the power of quality free content and the product launch strategy.

Reaching Out

Another lost art, and again something that Chris firmly believes was paramount to his success, was reaching out to media outlets and A-list bloggers from the minute that he launched his blog. Sure, it's hard to gain the confidence required to send an email to Seth Godin or Chris Brogan, but the worst they can say is no. There's no harm in that. In our experience, we've found that most bloggers will be more than happy to help in any way they can, so long as you aren't asking for too much and you approach them in the right manner.

Chris got help early on by paying popular consultants Chris Garrett (also featured in this book) and **Men with Pens** to critique his blog and help him perfect his design. This does two things:

1. The publicity you get from being featured on an A-list blog can bring a lot of traffic to your blog. You also get a link to your site, something that Chris believes is more important than making money.
2. You get honest feedback about how to improve your site in order to make it more attractive. Just make sure that you actually implement the changes as soon as you can afford to.

As far as reaching out to media properties and bloggers goes, building these relationships might take time, but will pay off for you down the road. Darren Rowse might not be able to pitch your product right now, but he'll remember your name. You never know when they'll send some love your way.

Aside from that, don't forget to do the same for the people below you. The little things that Chris does, like responding to 100 emails per day, commenting back on his blog, and replying to fans on Twitter helps him seem like one of us. If you become the guy or gal that isn't approachable, then you will have a hard time building relationships.

Chris calls these actions his "5 Daily Marketing Actions," but he tries not to stop at 5. Here are some other daily actions that he recommends pro-bloggers take to expand their reach and build their influence:

- Send out review copies of your products
  Always be thinking about the next phase of your plan
  Compose at least 1 guest post per month for another A-List blog
  Become proficient in as many skills as you can in order to improve your brand and marketing efforts
  Spend time building links, the "currency of the Internet"
  Track your stats on a spreadsheet so you can see what you are doing well and where you have room to improve
  Comment on other blogs
  Spend time on other social networks, such as Linked In and Facebook
- Always be co-creating and working with others in order to leverage your time and your abilities

Although the look and feel of Chris' journey might inspire you to follow suit, Chris wanted to stress that you shouldn't copy him. Instead, you should be following your own vision and doing your best to be you. This means you need to discover your own distinct brand and travel on your own distinct journey.

At the moment, upon the release of his latest guide "Yoga for the Social Web – Using Social Media as a Force for Good," Chris says that he is earning around $5,000 to $8,000 per month, most of which is profit, without having to sacrifice his travel time. He is working hard on his upcoming book, which is set to publish in September of 2010. As for getting that book deal, Chris said that he worked hard to find a literary agent that believed in him, and even harder to create a book proposal that was finally approved by the publisher.

As for Chris' future…it looks bright. He expects to be making over $10,000 per month consistently by the early portion of 2010, at which point he wants to focus on scaling his business to the next level. Although he was quiet on what he has to offer, knowing Chris, you can expect to be impressed.

The Original Geek

In those days we were making it up as we went along, and our only credentials were a dial up Internet account and an email address

The Original Geek

Chris Garrett

Many bloggers enter the blogging community because of their passion for writing, while others do so because of their interest in the technology of the Internet. Chris Garrett falls into the latter category.

Born in Calgary, Canada, Chris was brought up in Yorkshire in the UK and still lives there, although he and his family are planning a move back to Canada. The family in question is his wife, his daughter, a dog and a cat.

He first became involved in the Internet way back in 1994, when he was 20 years old, and when blogging hadn't even been heard of. These were the early days of Mosaic and Netscape and Chris was active on the rather geeky bulletin board scene, helping other people to understand the new technology. He started writing articles with tips to save him constantly having to rewrite the same answers over and over again. He'd then post links to his own site so that people could read the answers. Sound familiar? Chris was basically establishing, all those years ago, a strategy that all of us use to some extent today, to drive traffic to our blogs.

His first online project was to set up the network for the college he worked at. Bear in mind that these were the days of dial up connections, and he set up the college as an ISP, allowing local schools and libraries to access the Internet through the college system. In time he also developed the college's own intranet.

The project was a huge success and cemented his decision to make a career in this new world. You have to factor in that even Microsoft, at this time, weren't sure if the world wide web would ever take off, so Chris' early work was certainly pioneering, and laid the foundations of his vast knowledge of the online world.

"In those days we were making it up as we went along, and our only credentials were a dial up Internet account and an email address."

Having established himself in the industry, Chris then went through a period of ten years or so of working to create corporate websites for big companies. As well as the obvious skills of coding and creativity, this was a good learning process for him as he watched friends lose their jobs in various dot com crashes, and he witnessed the insecurity of working for someone else. Watching the mayhem around him, convinced him that he really wanted to work for himself, and in 2005 he set up his online media company, OMIQ.

Chris is much more than a blogger, he uses his skills and experience to provide companies and individuals with Internet marketing consultancy. With clients all over the world, he works a lot of hours, but enjoys the fact that he does so from home, when he chooses.

The Original Geek

"It is fair to say I would struggle to go back to commuting, having a boss, someone else telling me where and when I need to be in a certain place, what is on my to-do list"

In addition to the contracts he establishes with companies, he also offers advice for individual bloggers. His blog critiques are well known as a way to get the very best advice about how to move a blog onto the next level. Chris really delves deeply into the blog, highlighting where people are looking at a page, drawing out the actions that need to be focused on, and helping people to really push their blogs on towards their objectives.

Chris' overall strategy is quite different to many bloggers. His blogs aren't the key driver of his success – that comes from the consultancy, which is driven by his blogging. He offers a huge range of consultancy and advice to bloggers, from one hour telephone advice sessions, to a complete blog build or overhaul and even including writing top quality content to get a blog going. Overlaying all of this is his ability to focus on getting the reader to whatever the objective is.

His primary blog is Chrisg.com, where he posts about his craft, shares blog critiques and offers occasional products of his own for sale. He is not a frequent poster, averaging perhaps one a week on that particular blog, but he also consistently contributes posts to other blogs, both in his own stable (for example 5amtraveller.com) and on other blogs.

The content on *Chrisg.com* is full of solid advice and carries the benefit of his years of experience. One mantra you will hear from Chris all the time is the need to establish "Authority" as a blogger. Authority is what it takes to be taken seriously as a trainer or coach of other people, and Chris has made this area of blogging his own. He set up the **Authority Blogger Forum**, a site with a huge membership, and one which is a terrific learning resource for bloggers. And occasionally he opens the doors to his well respected **Authority Blogger** course.

One of the strategies Chris advocates for creating authority is to ensure that a blog uses what he calls "Flagship Content." This is "big" content that acts as anchors to a blog, attracting volume traffic and cementing the blog's brand, authority and position in the blogosphere. Chris has created a whole E-Book on the subject and gives it away to people who subscribe to the email list. There's a wonderful sentence in the book that sums up this approach. *"As busy web users we want one trusted resource that fully answers our question, in language we understand, in a place we can easily find."*

Chris became extremely well known in blogging circles when he co-authored the book, **Problogger - Secret for Blogging Your Way to a Six Figure Income,** with Darren Rowse. The book pulls together a lot of the learning that has been posted on Darren's

The Original Geek

Problogger site over the years and is a classic example of creating authority by publishing a bestselling book.

In terms of his own products, he is currently focusing on selling an E Book which is called ***Blogging for Business,*** and it's a great manual for people in conventional businesses who feel it's time they had a blog site to allow them to interact better with their clients and potential clients.

His career and profile have blossomed in the new age of social media, particularly on Twitter, where he has built up a huge following with his interesting, helpful and often funny observations. He's adopted the Web 2.0 mantra of social engagement as his own, and he makes connections all over the web using the plethora of tools available to help that happen. He describes his main focus now as being his desire to "engage people."

Chris talks extensively about his role models and lists Bill Gates, Richard Branson and Steve Jobs as people he admires, but he is also at pains to point out that he watches those around him in his own industry and learns a lot from other bloggers.

In terms of advice for new bloggers, he suggests that they should find something they are passionate about, with a ready-made audience, in a topic that they can make their own. One of his current projects reflects that. He's working on a social media workbook, which seeks to get feedback from people about what they want to know about social media. In return, he gives them answers, access to great content and free downloads. You can be sure there's a new book or product which will spin out of this research, but Chris is tight lipped about it at the moment!

During our interview with him, some of his character emerged when we asked at what point he knew he had become successful. Now bear in mind that he has a massive audience, has earned a good living on line for many years, and has written a bestselling book.

His answer was that he sees success as a process and not a result.

Chris on: Failing

Chris is not afraid of failure, and takes it as a natural consequence of being in a cutting edge industry. He's quite happy to admit that he fails all the time! *"Fail fast, fail often, and learn from your mistakes."*

Chris on: Success

He defines success not in monetary terms, but in life terms. *"To me success is about living the life that you want to live, waking up happy, and being with the people you want to share that life with.*

Everything else is a consequence or a means to that end."

He also describes the moment when he made the decision to branch out on his own. He says that yes, his income did go up, but that his lifestyle improved a thousand fold.

Managing multiple goals and tasks

Chris uses mind maps a great deal as a way to graphically illustrate his thoughts, and like most bloggers, he's pretty fluid with his working style. He's only recently adopted the process of writing goals and he found that useful to lay out a calendar for the next couple of years.

Unusually for a blogger, he's not heavily into tightly focused objectives. He believes you never know what's around the corner and that you should keep an open mind for the next opportunity.

Income

He made a decision some years ago not to share the details of his income with his readers, and I'm aware that he doesn't even reveal details of all the various blogs and businesses he does have some involvement with. This is in direct contrast to many bloggers who share lots of details and whose lives are an open, on-line book.

Summary

It's interesting that Chris goes against the grain in many areas when compared to other bloggers. A key difference is that he is essentially running a conventional consultancy business, which is supported by the blogs, rather than a business purely based on income from blogging itself.

His strengths are in harnessing his keen observation skills to adapt the medium to his own needs. Despite entering the industry so early, he has moved with it and has embraced social media to his great benefit.

- Chris believes in creating flagship content for a blog, which will keep drawing in new visitors via search.

  He majors on creating authority by establishing your credentials as an expert in the niche.

  He teaches that everything we do on a website should be focused on the reader and more importantly in taking the reader to a predefined objective.

  He advocates the strategy of creating networks in forums, via social media, and in offering those new network contacts free help and advice.

- He doesn't believe in having goals that are too rigid, preferring to retain the ability to react to a new market or opportunity

A Master of Networking

The big change in my blog's traffic came when I switched from writing about what interested me, and moved into what would help others

A Master of Networking

Chris Brogan

Chris Brogan is probably the first name most bloggers come up with when asked "Which blogs do you read?" With his soft voice, and lyrical prose, the blogger from Boston has become a household name.

Chris is simply one of the world's best users of all types of social media. He has emerged as new media's brightest star, and has built a brand and a platform for a whole new media business as well as creating a New York Times bestselling book. Chris Brogan is arguably social media's biggest player, so let's examine how he works and what he does.

These days, his life seems to consist of a constant round of speaking engagements, conference attendances, book signings, and all the other trappings of an Internet celebrity. But he has traveled a long road, and in common with our other featured bloggers, his work rate inspires awe. It surprised me to learn that his background is technical – Chris spent 16 years working in telecommunications, and during that time was involved with hardware and software design as well as managing various projects, including building data centers and the acquisition of other businesses. He spent most of his time with **Nynex**, who are now **Verizon**.

He first started blogging way back in 1998, before the word had even been invented – it was still called journaling then. It means that Chris has been blogging for eleven years! His first blog was simply a website, with a table where he would write the date in the left hand column, and the post in the right. Then he'd cut and paste it for the actual post.

Over the last ten years the blog has become essential reading for everyone involved in the social space, but it's very different to the conventional "How to" or "news" blog. Chris posts almost every day, and sometimes more than once a day, but his posts are thought-provoking and often contain as many questions as they do answers. Brogan has created a blog that actually delivers on the concept of "Learner-centered training."

When I interviewed him he made a point that really struck me: *"The big change in my blog's traffic came when I switched from writing about what interested me, and moved into what would help others. That change made the world of difference. I get lots more traffic now that I'm equipping others."*

His writing style is considered and thoughtful – which I find at odds with his technical background. His persona strikes me as a kind of benevolent, helpful uncle, and it is this that has enabled him to create a huge, and extremely loyal community around his brand.

A Master of Networking

Approachability

One thing that really distinguishes Brogan from other new media stars is his amazing approachability.

He's only recently taken on his first executive assistant, and that's his mother ,Diane. But even now, he answers almost all of his own email, and he happily agreed to contribute to this project, even though he was in the middle of a mammoth book tour at the time.

This extends to twitter, where a huge proportion of his tweets are replies to pretty much anyone who "talks" to him. Chris Brogan "owns" Twitter, often being ranked in the top 10 Twitter users by Twitter Grader. Ignoring conventional celebrities, Chris is probably the best user of Twitter on the planet, and he very, very rarely promotes any of his own work via the medium. His statistics are simply amazing:

- He follows almost 100,000 people
- He is followed by almost 110,000 people
- He has tweeted over 55,000 times!

Chris joined Twitter in October of 2006, so let's put that last statistic into perspective – he has tweeted over 50 times a day since then, an incredible amount considering the time he spends writing, speaking, and travelling. All of this has contributed to a simply huge amount of authority on Twitter. When Chris tweets or retweets, the Twitter world listens!

His blog enjoys huge traffic, and is ranked number one on the *Ad Age Power 150*, with over 35,000 subscribers. And Chris has never been shy of admitting that he blogs for income as well as to build a platform for his other businesses and activities, but he doesn't go overboard with it, and is extremely careful about disclosing any affiliations. The only overt advertising on the blog is for the *Thesis* blog theme, which he uses and is happy to recommend, and for *Blue Sky Factory* email marketing and *Rackspace Web Hosting*. Again, he uses both to great effect. He's also an avid reader, and regularly reviews books on his blog and on YouTube, linking to Amazon via affiliate links.

Interestingly, although Chris is open about the fact that he seeks to earn income from his work, he is also a firm believer in the "free" model for blogging, and has even gone so far as to license all his blog work under Creative Commons, allowing people to freely share his words. But the direct monetization is a very small part of the story, so let's examine how Chris has used the blog as a platform for his other ventures.

New Marketing Labs

Chris is the president of *New Marketing Labs,* a thriving company which helps conventional businesses understand new media and how to build relationships with their customers through it. *NML* has

A Master of Networking

an impressive client list, including companies like *PepsiCo, Sony* and *Microsoft.* And the list is growing all the time as people see Chris delivering on the *NML* promise day after day in his own work. By doing it himself, he superbly demonstrates that his company can do the same for others.

Chris and *New Marketing Labs* stress that companies first have to listen to the conversation that is going on in their marketing space, and then start to interact with the community. With this strategy, and by building a very strong team around him at *NML*, he has created one of the most successful new media marketing agencies.

PodCamps

Chris was a co-founder of the whole *PodCamp* idea. *PodCamp* started with its first conference in 2006, in Boston. The idea was to create a conference for people interested in knowing more and sharing more about their new media experiences. Since then *PodCamps* have been held all over the world including such far flung places as Brazil, Spain and Ireland.

The concept is that they should, where possible, be free to attend, and that all financials must be disclosed. They aren't a way to earn money for Brogan, but they are yet another amazing brand builder for him.

Speaking

Spinning out of **PodCamp** and all his other work, Chris has established a reputation as a fine public speaker, and he is in huge demand for any conference relating to social media. His presentation style is somewhat like his blogging style – he doesn't give answers, but seeks, through questions, to lead people to find their own answers. Unlike many speakers, he uses the minimum of notes and slides, and will adjust each presentation according to the level of comprehension and feedback he gets from the audience.

Looking at his speaking schedule would suggest that this is one of the most lucrative areas of his burgeoning businesses, and remember that the authority to offer this service has been built on a simple blog!

Inbound Marketing Summit

This is another collaborative effort, this time with Justin Levy. **Inbound Marketing Summit** is essentially a series of conferences for business people who want to understand the social media space better.

Each event has an impressive line-up of speakers, including people like Gary Vaynerchuk and Tim Ferris, with sponsorship and support from companies like **Mashable** and **Hubspot**. With sponsor-

A Master of Networking

ship at that level, and with attendance prices from $695 to over $1200, it should be assumed that these are quite profitable ventures.

Book Deals

Chris launched *Trust Agents* during 2009, a book he co-authored with Julien Smith. It was a text-book example of how to launch a book using a blog as the launch platform. *Trust Agents* quickly became a New York Times best seller and is now already a standard work for anyone involved in social media circles, or hoping to use social media to market a conventional business.

The book shares Chris' experience with social media, demonstrating how to use the web to build influence, how to improve authority, and as the name suggests, how to create trust. *Trust Agents* has managed to straddle the genres of "business handbook" and "great read" in a way few books have before. Some businesses have bought hundreds of copies to give out to staff, and many people in the social media community have purchased it to learn some of Chris' secrets.

One of the key tenets of *Trust Agents* is that to become a really successful brand or individual in the social media space, you need to offer people value, and make strong connections. If you can connect with as many people as possible, in as many ways as you can, and simply give them something, your brand or reputation will grow.

The most innovative section of the book, and the one which really moves the game forward, is the concept of "Agent Zero."

This is the point at which, having built up trust and authority via social media, one moves to simply connecting other good people with each other. And this seems to be the stage Chris is at in his own journey. He is the original Agent Zero.

I mentioned the launch process, which we should examine in a little detail. Chris and Julien started talking about *Trust Agents* months before the launch on their own blogs, and they also created a site and a community specifically for the book. Those of us who work in social media were well aware of the book and the impending launch for a long time.

On launch day Chris, appealed directly to his readers and subscribers. The message was simple: "We've been working on this book for a year, for you. I've been giving you plenty for free for a long time now. I'm hoping to get paid now, and buying *Trust Agents* is a good way for you to pay me." I've paraphrased it, but that was what Chris was telling us. It was enough to get me, and many, many other people to buy the book.

He then embarked on an amazing whirlwind tour of the United States, and seemed to be everywhere at once. But each

A Master of Networking

time he tweeted his location, he was able to gather an army of people to any location for his book signings. The whole launch process was a perfect demonstration of the concept of being a Trust Agent.

Failure

It would be easy to surmise from all this that Chris' rise has been straightforward, but that isn't the case. He's no stranger to failure: *"I fail quite often. There are posts that go nowhere. I just pick it up and go somewhere new."*

One new direction is in using video on the blog, something he really only started doing over the last year. It has had a big impact and has tapped into a new stream of readers he previously wasn't reaching.

Advice

Chris is happy to share advice with new bloggers. One of the things he repeats often is that bloggers need to find their own voice, their own style of blogging, and that they need to have fun with it. *"Try not to write me-too posts, but instead, add your own unique voice to the mix."*

He talks about having moved from being *"a guy who writes about things, to a guy who writes about things and also gets contracts from really big Fortune 100 companies."* But he makes no bones about the fact that he has to work extremely hard for his success, and he spends most weeks travelling, often getting up in the early hours to write blog posts.

At the time I interviewed him for this book, he was working on a project on his blog called "How to be an overnight success." It's one that he turned into a series after some really positive feedback from readers. It's a tongue in cheek look at how hard he has had to work, and for how many years, to have become an "overnight" success. It's typical Brogan – conversational, funny, interesting, but with a strong message that gets beneath the superficial humor.

In the series, he talks at length about the importance of his family to him, and despite his crazy schedule, he always makes time to be with the family. His wife is a strong supporter and is involved in every decision he makes.

Connecting

It's really interesting talking about connecting with Brogan. He dislikes the whole "Business card" exchange process at conferences, and he tells a story about one conference when he had

A Master of Networking

about 800 cards thrust at him, and once filtered, he ended up throwing away about 760 of them. Only forty were actually of interest, people he was likely to do business with, or people he knew anything about.

He makes the point that social media has to be about creating meaningful connections, and he derides the way that for some people it has become about chasing ever increasing numbers. And he bears this out with his own work – he really does connect with his vast army of readers and Twitter followers. He gives this advice to aspiring bloggers who want to collaborate in some way with an A-Lister. *"Get to know people, start a conversation with them, and be helpful. That breaks the ice, not handing them a piece of cardboard with your name on it."*

Point of Attention

One piece of advice he gives anyone involved in any kind of Internet marketing is that social media is all about reacting at the "point of attention." He cites an example, using Twitter. He's in Seattle, and the car due to collect him hasn't shown up, and he has an appointment at **Microsoft.** He's contacted by someone on Twitter who has a nationwide contact service for cars. It's the point of attention, and he's interested – of course he is! But if that guy had contacted him some weeks earlier, the service would have been of no interest to him at all.

And this, Chris feels, is the way businesses can really leverage the power of social media. By listening, they, and we bloggers, can establish when people are at the point of attention.

Let's imagine you sell an E book which helps give people advice about shopping in Florida. Set up a Twitter search for people using the term "Holiday in Florida" and you'll quickly see tweets from people planning holidays to the area. Don't pile in with "I have a great E-Book you can buy", but help them, offer them some free advice, or simply tell them that you're happy to help. Once you've dispensed your free advice, then you can tell them a little about your book.

Chris advocates spending most of your time on social media simply listening to the conversation, and setting up appropriate searches on topics of interest wherever you can.

The Future

We can expect more books from Chris. He's currently working on a solo project, and will be teaming up with Julien Smith on some kind of follow up to *Trust Agents*, and we can expect to see him continue on the conference circuit.

A Master of Networking

New Marketing Labs will continue to grow and earn new contracts, and I would expect to see his role in that business expanding during the next few years.

I asked Chris how he measures his success, and his answer was really quite illuminating. *"Success to me is helping others move the needle on their own goals and interests."* For me, that sums up Chris Brogan in a sentence.

Summary

Once again we can see some common factors coming out of the Chris Brogan story: Hard work and passion. In common with every single blogger we have interviewed for this book, Chris has an incredible capacity for hard work. Even now, riding the crest of a wave of success, we can see video of him recorded at 4AM en route to another day of travelling across the country to spend time with people.

His passion is not as overt as, for example, Gary Vaynerchuk's, but it's evident in the way he speaks, the way he writes and in his whole work ethic. On the face of it, he's one of the least commercial of our bloggers, but I suspect he's actually one of the most successful in that respect, and there's no doubt that the immense brand he has created around himself will provide a long term sustainable income for him and his family.

And you know what? He's a really nice guy too!

The Brazen Blogger

"I'm in a board meeting. Having a miscarriage. Thank goodness, because there's a fucked-up 3-week hoop-jump to have an abortion in Wisconsin"

The Brazen Blogger

Penelope Trunk

Penelope is a fascinating character, and has achieved a great deal of fame and some notoriety in recent years as one of the world's most read bloggers. I hate to use clichés, but her style really is unique.

If you suspected that Penelope Trunk is a pen name, you'd be right. Time Magazine assigned the name to her when she became a columnist with them, and she gradually became known as Penelope as her fame spread. When she stopped writing for other people, it made no sense not to capitalize on her previous efforts, so she adopted the name as her own.

Let's start by examining where she came from and how she got started. Her first "job" after college was as a professional beach volley ball player. Then, after a spell studying creative writing, during which a boyfriend kindly taught her HTML, she landed a position with a large company, running their online marketing business. She stayed with this until the end of the 1990's, when she reverted to her first love, which was, and continues to be writing.

Ever the entrepreneur, she was also founded a couple of Internet startups, and is today working on her third, Brazen Careerist, but we'll talk more about that later.

A seminal moment for Penelope came when she was living in New York, and was standing at the bottom of The World Trade Center when the buildings collapsed. She tells the full story of the horror on her blog, and it makes for compelling reading. She has written several times on the subject and described in detail her experience and the months of follow-up. Her description of the actual collapse and the effect on herself and the people around her at the time is one of the most compelling eye witness stories I have read of the event that changed the world. And it changed Penelope's world as well.

In the aftermath, she decided, with her then husband, to move out of New York and take stock of her life, returning to writing as her main career. While writing a column, which was being syndicated to over 200 newspapers, it dawned on her that she was helping to build other people's brands though her work, and it was that which persuaded her to start a blog – the opportunity to create a brand around herself and to build her own huge platform of readers and fans.

That blog is now at the heart of everything she does, and it has more than 40,000 subscribers. On the surface, the blog is offering career advice and also supports Penelope's business <u>Brazen Careerist</u>, which is a career management tool, aimed squarely at generation Y - those born between 1976 and 1980.

But dig through the archives and you'll find posts about her divorce, handling her kids, having a miscarriage and most recently her

The Brazen Blogger

marriage proposal from the boyfriend we only know as "The farmer." It's full of the most personal detail, and is truly an online journal, written with amazing candor. Penelope doesn't pull any punches at all, and it's that honesty which has made her blog compulsive reading for so many people, myself included.

Reading her blog is like reading someone's personal diary. It can have you laughing, crying and cringing, often in the same post. The on / off saga of the relationship with the farmer has been the best online soap opera, and promises to continue to provide entertainment now that the couple are getting married, although recent posts suggest that this may not still be happening - you'll have to read the blog yourself for the latest! Penelope's relationship with the farmer's family looks like it may create a great deal of interest for all of us in the future...at least from a storytelling point of view.

"That Tweet"

Often seeming to court controversy, Penelope is rarely out of the headlines, both online and off line. She recently received a great deal of criticism for sending the following tweet out:

"I'm in a board meeting. Having a miscarriage. Thank goodness, because there's a fucked-up 3-week hoop-jump to have an abortion in Wisconsin."

This created a furore in the US press, and rolled a few weeks later over to the British press, who took a typically "High Ground" stand over the subject.

I don't believe for a moment that there was any cynicism involved on Penelope's part – it's just the way she is – but it sure was good for business, having several TV and radio spots, and links to her sites all over national newspapers. Interestingly, she used the publicity to create debate around the whole subject of abortion, and at the same time educate many people, myself included, who believed that a miscarriage is a single event, rather than a drawn out process.

I asked Penelope if the people around her ever had a problem with their lives being openly discussed, and she explained to me that through her column and then her blog, it had always been the same. So people knew what to expect when they became a part of her life.

Unconventional

Her blog is not typical of other successful examples we've used in this book.

Her posting is inconsistent, doesn't stay focused on any particular niche, isn't monetized in any traditional way, and doesn't

The Brazen Blogger

employ any clever tricks or widgets – it's simply a home for her writing.

Despite all of that, it has achieved huge success, on the quality of the writing and the strength of the personality behind it. You may occasionally find an advertisement on there, but the bulk of the income comes from a syndication deal, allowing newspapers to take content when they want to, and believe me, that's lucrative. She earns five figures per month purely from these syndication deals.

Platform

Above all, the blog is a platform for her brand and acts as a marketing tool for her business. The blog has documented in detail the start up of *Brazen Careerist*, her personal issues with colleagues, and most recently her decision to appoint a new CEO, allowing her to focus on her blog and continuing to build her brand.

The *Brazen Careerist* site is a superb example of Web 2.0 in action. It moves the whole career process from the rather stuffy "See a job advertised, send a résumé" process to a more natural networking system. Applicants create a profile on the site, where they can upload their résumés, and can also add links to their blogs and Twitter feeds and post their ideas and thoughts. It means that both potential employers and co-workers can get a much better feel for a future employee than they can from a letter or telephone conversation. It's turning employment on its head, with companies using the site to actively seek out new workers. **Brazen Careerist** was brilliantly described by **Fast Company** as "Twitter meets Facebook, meets Linked in, meets generation Y......and it's about time."

It's still in both beta and startup mode, but has some substantial funding in place. It will be interesting to watch how the site will eventually be monetized.

Penelope's use of Twitter is interesting. Unlike many bloggers, she has never used the platform directly to promote her blog. In fact she probably uses Twitter the way it was originally designed to be used. She really does use it as a micro-blogging platform – with a single tweet every few days. She has a knack of getting the most information into 140 characters and at the same time often being humorous. Each is like a mini blog post.

Advice

In terms of advice for new and learning bloggers, Penelope once again takes a different path. She eschews many of the conventional notions of SEO, AdSense and Digg, suggesting that writers should concentrate on creating a conversation on their blog. She uses many links in her posts to make sure she is entering into the conversation that already exists on any given topic, rather than "talking at" her readers about it. In fact, she told me she often spends longer inserting the links in her posts than she does actually writing them!

She also advises bloggers to avoid starting new blogs. It's a common theme for a blogger to be constantly redesigning their sites, adjusting their niche, then to suddenly announce a new blog on a new topic. Penelope feels this is something that should be avoided – by doing so a blogger will lose the community already built up around the blog, the connections, and the brand building. Instead she suggests that bloggers should stick with what they've started and "explore the edges" of their niche. She says blogging is about *"What you are thinking,"* not your topic, and feels bloggers shouldn't be afraid to move outside of their regular points of reference. She goes on: *"Blogging is about establishing your brand as your whole self"* and when you and your values change, they should do so on your blog, rather than by starting a new one. For her, blogging should be treated in part as a voyage of self-discovery.

Asperger's

One constant theme running through her writing is her reference to Asperger's Syndrome, from which Penelope suffers. She doesn't suffer in the comedy way portrayed on television, but from a more subtle form of the illness. Sufferers commonly have a high intelligence, but often lack social skills and the ability to empathize with other people – to "read" them. This could be considered to be a huge liability in an entrepreneur, but characteristically, Penelope has developed coping mechanisms along with her work colleagues, and the fact that she has spoken so openly about it, means that most of her business contacts are aware of her situation. Interestingly her blog ranks very well for any search on Aspberger's and by writing so much about it, she has helped to bring discussion about it into the open.

Summary

One thread that kept coming up during my interview with Penelope is that she feels quality of writing is absolutely essential to a blog becoming mainstream. She cited several other blogs, including purely technical ones that she lists among her favorites. They all had top quality writing in common. She believes it's an essential key to success as a blogger. Her own writing meets that criteria, and she told me I would be surprised how much time and effort she puts into each blog post, often spending hours working through an argument and cross referencing her data on other sites. She measures her own success in terms of the conversations she starts on her blog, and it's common for her posts to get more than 100 comments. One celebrated post has over 700 comments! She loves it when people choose an opposing view, as long as they have researched her links to other data and really understand the point. There are many heated exchanges in her comments, but what she has created is a platform for debate on a huge variety of subjects.

Once again, with Penelope Trunk, we see a totally different approach to blogging and earning income. And it's interesting that each of our featured bloggers have achieved their success in different ways.

For Penelope, writing is the passion, and the blog acts almost as a release for her and as a continuation of the columns she has been writing for years. It's main purpose is to act as a vehicle for her to write and to build her personal brand, which in turn builds her business brand and acts as a marketing platform. It's a seemingly complicated mix, but it works, and it works because the joy of writing is behind everything. I suspect that rich or poor, win or lose, Penelope will simply continue writing, and the fact that she can generate a substantial income by doing so is simply a beneficial by product, rather than the primary objective.

Straight Shooting Six Figure Blogger

Help your audience solve real-world problems and achieve real-world goals. IF you do that, they'll take a sword for you

Straight Shooting Six Figure Blogger

David Risley

David is a consummate online professional, and has been earning his living via the Internet since before he left college. He grew up in the Tampa Bay area of Florida, and continues to live there with his wife, and daughter, with another child on the way. He even met his wife via the Internet, back in 2005.

David studied information systems management at college, and while there he began earning his first income online. When it was time to graduate, he already realized that he had found his career, and while his peers set off to find jobs, he began a smooth transition to running his own business.

His first online project, and a site he still owns and runs today, was www.pcmech.com. Way back in 1997, he created the website and without even knowing what a blog was, he effectively designed one. *PCMech* helps people "get their geek on" and began as a tech site to help people understand how computers work and how to get the best from them. In common with so many of the bloggers we interviewed, he started out coding his own site using HTML – modern tools like WordPress must seem so easy to these guys!

The new site quickly captured the imagination of readers, following what we now know to be a classic blog format – giving lots of good quality, free information away, whilst generating decent revenue from advertisers.

This took place during the dot com bubble, and within three years David was made a substantial offer for the business, with him continuing to run the company. Wooed by the large sums involved, he accepted, shortly before the bubble burst.

Revenue from advertisers quickly dried up, and David learned a lesson that has stayed with him to this day. He never leaves all his eggs in one basket, preferring to spread the risk with multiple streams of income. His reaction to the problems was typical – instead of folding, he looked for a solution. The answer was to reformat content he had already written and sell it via a CD. Effectively, he had created a very early E Book. The CD sold for $21.99, and he furiously took orders, wrote envelopes and licked stamps to keep his business afloat.

The company who had bought the business were also in trouble and they had already stopped making the agreed payments to David, so he simply removed the site from their servers, wrote them a letter telling them they were in breach of contract and offering to "see them in court." In the event they didn't respond, and David was back in control at *PCMech*.

The whole experience had a profound effect on him, and the seeds of his business style and approach had been sown. He had seen the power of creating his own product and marketing it through a mailing list to a targeted audience.

For the next couple of years, David got **PCMech** firmly back on track, building an audience of more than 20,000 subscribers and getting over 850,000 page views per month. He also launched a premium membership site, where members could get additional information for a monthly charge, and he took on other writers to keep the site running well while he concentrated on marketing the business and his next project which was www.davidrisley.com

Up until this point he had been the "invisible man" quietly working away and earning a genuine six figure income online. But nobody knew who he was or how he was doing it.

Putting learning back into the community

It was time to build a brand around his own name and to share the knowledge he had built up over the previous few years. He had technical expertise, he understood how to market a website, how to create a community and how to make products and sell them to that community. But he had also been studying the Internet marketers, and he realized that adding their techniques to the way bloggers can build traffic and authority could be a formula for huge success.

"I made a trip to the home of Internet marketer Harris Fellman, just outside Phoenix, AZ. I went there for a retreat with several other Internet marketers. We did what is called "hotseats", where a person will talk about his business challenges and the entire group would help brainstorm solutions. I told them about my tech blog and my plans to launch a membership site for it. When they heard my traffic numbers, they were dumbfounded. None of them had that much traffic. What it showed me is that marketers make crappy bloggers, but bloggers make crappy marketers. When you combine them, good things happen. Those people there were making much more money than I, but their blogs sucked. What they clearly understood was marketing and persuasion, and building actual businesses."

For David, the new launch meant getting back to basics. Months of hard work followed, during which he focused on getting really good content onto the site, building his own brand and creating some credibility for himself in the niche. He found Twitter to be a great medium for doing so, has established himself as a big player there, and as an authority on the subject of how to give and get the best from the micro blogging platform.

Maximizing his experience as someone who had been earning money online, and combining that with the hard work referred to above, gave _DavidRisley.com_ a quick start, and the site built a strong following. The "How to make money online" niche is a very crowded space, but whilst his site offers great advice to all bloggers, he has "lasered" in on one segment of the niche – already established bloggers who want to take their blogs to the next level and start to generate a decent income from them.

He was able to use his experience and expertise as someone who had been successful for some time, and he famously told the world about how he earned over $12,000, whilst on a cruise with his wife, by selling his premium membership to **PCMech**. That kind of publicity and social proof is priceless.

Style

His writing is excellent and is perfectly suited to the blogging medium, using short sentences and a conversational style. He's also extremely forthright, and states his opinion boldly and firmly. There is no-nonsense and it's very easy to understand his message. You can sense his frustration at times – he wants his audience to take action and to treat their blogging as a business, and that frustration is borne out of seeing so many people read and talk about what they are going to do, without actually doing anything.

David's own site has become a place of learning and ideas,

with clear and easy to understand posts coming out almost every weekday. Along with the usual stuff about social media and traffic building skills, it also acts as a conduit for David's thoughts and opinions, as well as a strong base for the community to interact via the lively comments section.

Income

Having established the new site with a decent readership and an email list that was growing, it was time to actually earn some money. The first step was to create a high quality report "Six figure blogger blueprint" which David offered to anyone signing up to his email list. The report established his credibility by telling his story and giving detailed information about his success and earnings. Once again, a free report, or manifesto was used to generate interest and subscribers.

The next step was "3 day money", a short course, which taught the basics of using Internet marketing techniques to create an online income for bloggers.

And then David launched his flagship product – **Blog Master's Club**. **BMC** is a membership program packed full of content that will help bloggers move to the next level in their businesses. There are modules on every area of blogging, delivered in several formats, and the whole thing is backed up by a forum where David spends a lot of his time. David is a strong advocate of this kind of membership site, and we can expect to see more of this type of product from him. The course is six months long and members who complete the training will then retain access to all the materials and the forum for life, and David will constantly be adding new and updated content to the member areas.

Along side his own products, David offers a few affiliate programs to his subscribers. He's a big advocate of the *AWeber* email management system, and he has offered courses on behalf of other bloggers like Yaro Starak, but only if he values the content and feels they provide value.

Transparency

David believes in transparency and in "being yourself" as a blogger; he's very happy to share his life with his readers. We know all about his family - photos and events are shared, and David is happy to share details of his income, seeing it as proof that he practices what he preaches. In 2008, his overall income from blogging was $141,000 and this year he'll earn close to $200,000. Although those are gross figures, the figures are proof that he is genuinely a "six figure blogger."

In common with every single person interviewed for this book, David extols the virtue of hard work. He works full time, normally from 0800 until 1800 each day, but he's been known to pull an all-nighter when a project is nearing completion. On the subject of work rate, he says "Remember, this is a business. Money doesn't appear out of the air – you need to work hard for it and work smart."

He believes in having clearly defined goals and distilling them down to a daily to-do list, and these are routines he has been using for years to great effect. He feels bloggers can easily be distracted by having so much information on hand via the Internet and that we all need clearly defined daily goals.

In terms of role models, Frank Kern and John Reese have been very influential influences on David's blogging career. Also, David reads and learns from other A-Listers, including Darren Rowse, John Chow ,and Yaro Starak. He also mentions Brian Clark and told me that his launch of Teaching Sells acted as the impetus for David's own Blog Master's Club.

Outside of the industry David's first role models were his parents, who he describes as having *"taught him the spirit of entrepreneurship by example."*

Advice

I asked him what advice he'd give to new bloggers, and he told me that:

- *Quality content your audience wants to read is paramount.*
- *Don't forget that you need to engage in marketing. You need to study the art of persuasion and how to create/sell products to your audience. Selling is only a dirty word if you want to make any money. If you do, then get over it.*
- *Build trust and understanding with your audience. You want them to know, like and trust you. You do that by consistently fostering communication and reality with them.*
- *Help your audience solve real-world problems and achieve real-world goals. IF you do that, they'll take a sword for you.*
  BE REAL. Never be fake. Be yourself. There is only one you, so there is no competition.
- *Remember, this is a business. Your blog is ultimately a lead generator. Create good content and do all the things good bloggers do. But, never forget that business requires selling. Always include a call to action and get your audience to do things.*

He added that to be a successful entrepreneur people also need to be efficient, trustworthy, and good at networking. He said that that they should: *"Help people. Help people even if you're not getting paid for it. Reciprocity ultimately comes into play. The karma comes back. If you can help arrange a deal to help two people mutually and you're not one of them... do it anyway."*

He also offers some solid advice about building a brand, suggesting bloggers should own their own domain, invest in some professional design and photography to convey the brand message, and "above all, be everywhere in the online space." He has certainly practiced the latter over the last 12 months, traveling to most conventions and meetings relating to blogging, and this has generated a huge number of fruitful contacts for him. He's also active in a Mastermind Group in Tampa and strongly advocates those kinds of groups for entrepreneurs to build up their networks.

David's strength as a teacher of how to make money online is that he has been doing it for so long, doing it consistently, and doing it well. In fact he's never done anything else! For nine years he's written great content, created communities and made products to sell to them. During that time, even during the dot com crash, he has been able to sustain himself and his family, buy houses and cars, and live the lifestyle of his choice.

He deserves his success and I suspect that future years will see his business continue to grow steadily upwards.

Straight Shooting Six Figure Blogger

Case Studies

Self Styled Dot Com Mogul

Every link on this blog is a paid link. If it is not a paid link, then it was an oversight on my part and it will become a paid link soon.

Self Styled Dot Com Mogul

John Chow

Perhaps no single pro blogger has been quite as successful or as notorious as John Chow has been for shamelessly monetizing every single aspect of his business.

Take a look at his blog disclosure policy below and you'll get a feel for what I mean.

To comply with the recent FTC ruling (not that I have to since this blog is not based in the USA) over bloggers getting paid to write stuff, I offer the following disclosure policy. If you're reading my blog, you should assume the following:

I make money from every post I put on this blog. If I'm not making money from every blog post, then it was an oversight on my part and it will be corrected soon.

Every link on this blog is a paid link. If it is not a paid link, then it was an oversight on my part and it will become a paid link soon.

Every product I write about on this blog, I get for free. If I didn't get it for free, then there was a miss-communication with the company that sent it and I will be billing them for the cost so the product becomes free. I make money from every tweet I send out on Twitter. If I didn't make money on the tweet, then it was an oversight on my part and it will be corrected soon.

If you email me, all of the information in your email is mine to do with as I please, such as exploit for financial profit, use as blackmail, or quote on my blog.

The T-shirts you see me wear at trade shows. I get paid to wear them. If I didn't get paid to wear them, then it means I ran out of paid shirts and had to wear a free one. In which case, I will go to the company that gave me the free shirt and ask them to sponsor it.

If something on the Net is making a lot of money, you can bet I will be in on it. If I'm not in on it, then it was an oversight on my part and it will be corrected soon.

Just because I get paid to blog, tweet, wear T-shirts, etc. does NOT mean I will give you or your company a positive review, blog post or endorsement. As a matter of fact, chances are pretty high that I might slam you.

Although John does a great job of playing the bad boy, the truth is that he does it because it works well.

It's this strategy of ruthless link building and monetization that helped him take his blog from earning $0 per month to over $40k per month.

And it was this achievement that helped him skyrocket to Internet fame and recruit a viewership of rookie bloggers that eagerly consumes every blog post, recommendation, and affiliate offer.

Self Styled Dot Com Mogul

The interesting part about John's pro blogging journey though is that he, like David Risley, got his start by creating a niche blog about various types of computer hardware and technology. In John's case, it was The Tech Zone (TTZ), which he founded in 1999 by borrowing computer hardware from local shops and creating reviews online.

Over time, he was able to grow a sizeable readership, which he monetized primarily with **Google AdSense** and a variety of affiliate sponsorships. **TTZ** operates a lot like Darren Rowse's *Digital Photography School,* which also drives traffic with niche content and monetizes with **Amazon** and *Google AdSense.*

As for John's notoriety, one of the things he is most noted for was being sent to the sandbox by **Google,** meaning that his blog was banned from the search rankings. John received the dreaded "Google slap" because he participated heavily in the process of buying and bartering links for the term "make money online." Although many try this technique, as John learned, there are few that don't get caught.

At that time, John's blog was still receiving a decent amount of traffic, but the Google slap allowed other blogs, like JohnCow.com to capitalize on John's misfortune. Taking it in stride and using other methods of getting traffic for the short term, John eventually got his search engine rankings back and climbed back to the top of the charts in the make money online niche.

Getting Traffic

No blogger can survive without traffic, and these days, getting a large amount of steady traffic is harder than it seems. However, John practically pioneered many of the more popular traffic strategies that do still work.

For instance, one of the first steps that John took to build his blog was to guest post for as many A-List blogs as he could. He also worked hard to recruit new views by commenting on other blogs, getting blog reviews, and doing smart SEO work.

Lastly, he understood the value of building a large email list, which he was able to do by using the traditional tactic of creating a free report to offer in exchange for someone's email address.

Spreading Your Assets

John is a master of monetization, but it's really not the way that he places ads or affiliate offers that do this for him, it's the way that he spreads his income throughout a variety of offers and networks.

For instance, John does a great job of referring new affiliates to popular ad publishers and affiliate networks, such as *Market Leverage*. He mentioned in an interview that he receives 5% of a new publisher's income if they sign up through his link, which means that he can build passive income without having to sell anything at all.

John is also paid to review websites and products, usually at a price of $500 per review, at which point he'll make even more money by adding an affiliate link within the post. As we mentioned earlier, he's not afraid to monetize anything, and you'll rarely see a blog post or newsletter published without an affiliate link of some kind.

If you take a look at his website, you'll see a huge amount of links, banner ads, and sidebar ads. In fact, one could argue that his blog contains more banners and advertisements than it does content. However, when you are receiving around 100k unique visitors per month, it is likely that you will have advertisers beating down your doors for a slice of that traffic.

This also brings up an interesting point, which is that John's blog is far from the most popular blog in the world. He's outranked by both *Copyblogger* and *Problogger,* but what he lacks in traffic he makes up for in monetization. He has the advantage of being in a niche that constantly recycles buyers, so he can continue to sell the same products every single day.

Like other people in the make money online niche, John has positioned himself in the perfect spot to sell these products because of his authority as a "dot com mogul." Although he stopped posting income reports to his blog in 2009, John was consistently making 30k-40k per month on this site alone. Combine that with what he makes with the **Tech Zone** and the **Ad Network** that he created for the **Tech Zone**, and you've got quite a decent monthly income that rookie bloggers are desperate to achieve.

Outsourcing

When John started his blog, he really didn't intend to make money with it. But once he realized that he had a new money maker, he made a smart business move by hiring people to handle his other websites so that he could focus all of his energy on JohnChow.com. He didn't stop there however, because soon he outsourced much of the process of content creation and management to his partner Michael Kwan. Even his ad company, **TTZ Media**, is fully automated.

This is where a lot of bloggers fail, and why many projects cannot be scaled to the size necessary for them to be successful. The only way to really let a project go is to remove yourself from the equation. When you do this, you give it room to breathe, and it frees you to work on new projects. Even if John sold his personal blog, it would be able to carry on because of the manner in which he's removed himself from it.

As a blogger, you need to think in terms of exit plans and of scalability. If you want to create a lifestyle that allows you to work from anywhere without being tied down, then you'll need to find a way to manage your blog so that it can be outsourced, and possibly sold, down the line.

If not, you will be tied to your blog and stuck every single day trying to create new content and new products. If you can't afford outsourcing right now, one of the easiest ways that you can do this is by asking for guest posts. You'll find that John often posts guest posts from other up and coming bloggers, which works to spell his efforts and help others share a bit of the spotlight.

In fact, many of the blogs listed in this book use a similar strategy, by either hiring an editor, taking frequent guest post submissions, or partnering with other up and coming bloggers. If this is a strategy that you seek to implement, then make sure you advertise your interest in accepting guest posts. Throw up a page that allows people to submit guest posts and then make sure to advertise that page via Twitter, Facebook, and your email newsletter.

Once you've reached the level of success that allows you to hire someone to help you out, do it, whether in an associate or senior editor capacity. This is where you can find time to create new and better products than those you currently offer. It's also how you can start new blogs or improve the ones you already own.

As for the making money part of the equation, if you don't have any products of your own, use John's strategy of linking to them in your blog posts. Although I wouldn't recommend featuring a product that isn't something you'd buy yourself, there's nothing wrong with doing a review from time to time. This is also where it becomes important to build an email list, as an email list is usually much more responsive than a blog post.

When you do start selling affiliate products, try to keep a buyer's list so that you can separate the tire kickers from the customers. You will find that your customers will be the ones that continue to buy from you, regardless of how often you promote new products. This is especially true when it is time to launch a new product, as your buyer's list alone can help you have a successful launch.

If you are looking to John Chow for inspiration or guerilla tactics, you probably won't find them. However, if you are looking for simple, but tried and true techniques for building an audience, monetizing that audience, and scaling a platform, then John is the perfect model. If nothing else, don't be afraid to be you. John might make a lot of money, but he's not afraid to rub your face in it. That's what works for him…that's John. Find your own angle and then work it until it becomes a successful platform. From there, the sky is the limit.

Self Styled Dot Com Mogul

The Internet's Brad Pitt

As people began to drift towards new media, they needed a place to go and find out about each new shiny on-line toy

The Internet's Brad Pitt

Pete Cashmore

Pete Cashmore is a fascinating character. He started Mashable in July of 2005, at the age of 20, from his parent's home in the north of Scotland. Within two years he was an Internet celebrity and *Mashable* was one of the world's biggest and most profitable blogs.

Pete was working as a web consultant when he came up with the idea for *Mashable*.

He was heavily into the social space, and felt there was a need for a site which would be useful to people who wanted to understand the new tools available to them. He embarked on an incredible posting spree, sometimes posting ten or twelve times a day, seldom less than seven, and although *Mashable* now employs several writers, Pete is still a regular contributor, and *Mashable* continues his prolific output. If ever there was a success story that epitomizes the adage that "content is King" then *Mashable* is that site.

Pete is the first to admit that his timing was a major factor in his success. When he started, social media was in its infancy, and nobody was predicting the huge impact it would have on the Internet generally or that it would become so mainstream.

He likens the time then to the dawn of the industrial revolution – he realized that something huge was about to happen, and all he needed was a computer to be part of it!

In the early days of the blog, Cashmore focused on building readership and creating a community around the blog, with no thoughts of monetization. And as people began to drift towards new media, they needed a place to go and find out about each new shiny on-line toy. *Mashable* quickly became that place, and a huge community formed around the site, as established members helped new people get their heads around Web 2.0.

The designers and developers of all the new applications quickly realized they could tap into this growing audience, and became active participants themselves, both working with the community and passing information and ideas to Pete to gain some publicity for what they were doing.

This in turn meant that *Mashable* established a reputation for being a breaker of news, and at the forefront of the social media game – both key features that continue to keep the site at the top of everyone's RSS feeds.

Realizing that he had something special building, Pete worked hard to establish *Mashable* not just as a website, but as a brand, and in some ways pioneered this for other websites. As well as all the obvious facets of branding like the site design and logo, Pete

The Internet's Brad Pitt

instigated a series of events billed "Mashable Meet ups" where he brought members of the community and industry together. These continue today, all over the world.

The site's first move towards monetization came in the form of sponsorship deals from industry organizations, and direct advertising slots quickly followed. Pete and *Mashable* have never been frightened of creating as much profit as possible from the site, and today it features a great deal of advertising in many forms, including *Google AdSense*. *Mashable* even has a job board which always has at least 50 jobs advertised in the industry......at $50 a month!

It's rumored that several significant offers have already been made to Pete to buy out *Mashable*, and he has steadfastly refused them all. Instead he has broadened the brand by using his own celebrity, almost in the way Richard Branson did previously with Virgin. Pete is now a regular on television and radio, and is often wheeled in as the "social media expert" when one is required. His youth, good looks, and a fantastic dress sense all help in attracting more readers, and Pete is excellent at getting plugs for the site every time he appears in any other media.

An extension of this has been the clever use of sponsorship to create more publicity for both the site and the industry. For example, Cashmore persuaded Microsoft to sponsor the Spark of Genius series on the site. Developers get a chance to showcase their new ideas,

Mashable gets to run the first stories about them, and therefore get an inside track as they grow, and the whole thing is paid for by **Microsoft Bizspark**!

The site's biggest growth was during 2007, when it effectively moved from being a blog to a full-on business. Several people were hired including a COO and a CTO to run the commercial and technical operations respectively. At this time Pete was spending a lot of time in San Francisco where he set up a home.

By now, a team of writers were producing a lot of the content, but Pete made sure he hired professional journalists who were not only able to embed in the community, but also keep an eye out for the scoop stories as well as finding the different angles that ***Mashable*** is famous for, and which keeps it ahead of the plethora of other sites springing up in the same niche.

The site went through a major rebranding in early 2008, with the byline changing from "All that's new on the web" to the simpler and more descriptive "The social media guide." At this time, Pete was also named as a Forbes "Top 25 Web celebrity." The transition from another blogger churning out content in a back room of his parent's house to a media mogul was complete.

He recently moved back to Scotland, as he found the pace in the US a little too much for him, but he regularly travels back there for various events and meetings, although he uses the latest tech-

The Internet's Brad Pitt

nology to stay in touch with his empire. He also works US time in Scotland, which must be strange, but he's accepted that he needs to be around when his biggest market is awake!

Mashable now enjoys a subscriber list of over 300,000 and close to 2 million Twitter followers. People are falling over themselves to write for the site, submit stories about their businesses (they get around 400 submissions a day) and I suspect it is one of the world's most profitable websites. In fact, when Cashmore was recently asked if that was the case, he simply smiled at the camera!

So how has he achieved so much, in such a short a time? I suspect Pete would be the first to admit that timing was a major factor. He was the right guy, in the right place, with the right interest and all at the right time. Here comes the but - he worked very, very hard in the early days. He was lucky enough to get in at the beginning of social media as we know it today. However, there were plenty of other people doing the same thing, and many had greater assets in terms of financing and people. Pete quickly recognized he couldn't match them in those areas, but he could in work rate.

So that's exactly what he did – he set out to blow people's socks off by carrying every single relevant story in his niche, every day. And he did it on his own in the early days. It's an inspiring story.

The Zen Marketer's Group

She's not only at the top of her game, but she's bringing the world with her

The Zen Marketer's Group

Shama Kabani

Would you believe me if I told you that I knew of a rising star in social media who has created a six figure full service online marketing firm from her house in less than a year, has been labeled by *Fast Company* as a "millennial master of the universe," has been featured in a handful of social media conferences across the country, and who is just 24?

Would it help if I told you that her eBook, *The Zen of Social Media*, sold so many copies that she had to pull it because she had publishers begging her for a book deal? I know, it's tough to believe, but Shama Kabani (formerly Shama Hyder) has rocketed so quickly to the top of the social media stratosphere that even she is amazed by the publicity.

For Shama, it started years ago when she became an empowerment coach, focusing on "Law of Attraction" (LoA) strategies and personal empowerment. From there, she found her rhythm as an online marketing consultant, at which point she formed The Marketing Zen Group, a full scale online marketing firm that focuses on social media branding and marketing.

Within a year, Shama had turned *The Marketing Zen Group* into a six figure business. What's interesting about that is that *The*

Marketing Zen Group operates completely online, meaning that she isn't isolated to an office, timezone, or location. Although she works with a great team of designers, developers, and copy gurus, she has managed to save money on overhead and operating costs by recruiting like-minded professionals to work from their own home.

Although I hadn't heard of Shama until I stumbled upon her eBook, *The Zen of Social Media*, you could tell just by listening to her speak that she was confident and on top of her game. Using her expertise in new media marketing, she found a way to energize business clients and help them reinvent their online campaigns. Furthermore, she used this expertise to market her own eBook, which sold so many copies that she was able to convince a publisher to sign her to a book deal. This is virtually unheard of in the information marketing era, as most eBooks are destined to a life of eBook readers and *Adobe Acrobat*.

What I find most impressive about Shama though, is that she was able to pull all of this off before her 25th birthday. She's not only at the top of her game, but she's bringing the world with her.

Shama.TV

So how did she do it? Was she just lucky enough to get a few clients to sing her praises? Did she use some kind of secret ninja tactic to recruit affiliates and build up hype? The answer to that of course is no. Instead, she simply followed the most logical path, which was to create a blog that could serve as a platform for her clients and her tightly knit community. With video as her medium of choice, she showcased her delightful personality, remarkable knowledge, and amazing expertise in a way that bought the trust and devotion of her following.

Shama has a knack for making the most of every opportunity, and her video blog is a perfect combination of relevant advice and subtle marketing. *Shama.TV* covers a wide range of new media topics that are extremely educational, especially for a business looking to get involved with Social Media. Shama is smart about that, because rather than being just another talking social media head, she's found a way to own her portion of the Internet by catering to both small business and large corporations, many of whom are still struggling for a meaningful approach to establishing a new media presence. By doing this, Shama has been able to separate herself from both the competition, and the rest of the community, which puts her on a high standing platform all by her lonesome.

Although Shama's video blog isn't what drives her income, like Gary Vaynerchuck, she uses it to fuel her brand. The blog is the platform that draws attention to her business. When a client hears her name, they'll head to Shama.TV, where they'll see that she isn't just someone trying to cash in on the new media hype. At that point, she has instant authority, which is how her business went from zero to six figures almost overnight.

Behind the Scenes

Now that we know the story, let's dig into the behind the scenes action to see what we can learn from Shama's rise to Internet fame. Upon doing a little Google research, once can see that Shama's story is an almost textbook case of how you can create a platform overnight.

1. She leveraged guest posting as a way to not only send traffic to her blog, but build creditability for her consulting firm. One of the blogs that she wrote for was the widely popular Freelance Switch, which has a readership of over 45,000 and a community of nearly 25,000 members.
2. Shama created a free report, called "101 Ways to Market Your Business," which she gave away on her website upon successful completion of an opt-in form.

It's been said time and time again that guest posting and giving away free content are two of the most successful strategies for developing an audience online, but for some reason, there are tons of bloggers that just don't buy in. It's not hype folks, it is a simple bricks and mortar strategy for blogging success.

Now, I don't want to marginalize Shama by saying that she doesn't have anything special to bring to the table, because she obviously has a lot of expertise. However, had she not been willing to share that expertise, for free, via her guest posts, free books, and videos, then she would probably still be trying to build her business to six figures. Instead, she's moving on to the next level, where she can use her maven status to create an even larger platform.

And she does that extremely well. There is nothing wrong with self-promotion, especially if you can back it up. Shama does it in a way that makes her seem larger than life. The pictures of her on Shama.TV are professional, just like the image she is trying to present. Her bio is tremendous, and she makes it incredibly easy for people to find out what she does and how they can bring her to the fight.

Too many bloggers are scared of their own identity, fearing that if they try to promote themselves, then they will come off looking like a snake oil salesman. But if you've got the goods, then why be afraid of selling them? Let's face it, there's nothing magical about Facebook or Twitter, but Shama's confidence level is addictive, and people want to be a part of what she does.

Let this be an example of how selling the story, your story, is just as important, if not more important, than selling the skill. You don't need to reach everyone, but if you can reach that part of the world that is captivated by your persona, then you can dominate your own portion of that niche. It doesn't matter if you are selling eBooks, consulting services, or knitted sweaters. More often than not, it's the story that sells, not the product.

The Young One

Michael has focused from the beginning on creating a community around his brand, and it's this strong community which provides him with his income

Michael Dunlop

Michael is another interesting character, who in many ways goes against the mold of the successful blogger. He's very young and he doesn't blog in the normal sense. His client base is all over the world, but he remains living in England, although he travels extensively in the United States.

The son of well known Internet marketer Barry, it was almost inevitable that Michael would carve an online career for himself from a young age. And it's to his credit that he has overcome dyslexia in order to do so.

His entrepreneurial flair first came to his parent's attention when he was just five years old. *"I want to own a shop when I grow up."* He declared. *"A toy shop?"* was his mother's reply. *"No, a superstore, like Tesco or Wal-Mart!"*

Like many youngsters, Michael's first online efforts were on eBay, where he quickly discovered he could make a good income simply buying and reselling goods. While his contemporaries were earning a few pounds doing paper rounds, he was already earning an excellent income.

He created his first website at age 16, and was immediately hooked on the excitement of pulling traffic in to his site from the vast outside world. This first website came out of a school project, where he and his classmates were running an imaginary company. The pupil who had been delegated to create a website used a very basic free site template, and Michael decided he could do a much better job himself. Teaching himself code, he created a much improved version and then he was on the road to a web based future!

Having learned the skills required to create a website, Michael started to think about what niche his first blog should focus on. The answer soon became obvious – it would be for and about young entrepreneurs, and Retireat21.com was born. This remains his flagship online platform, and Michael still just qualifies as he is only 20!

In setting up the blog he had some very clear goals:

1. He only wanted to work a few hours a day.
2. He wanted to create a passive income that would continue even when he stopped working.
3. He wanted to work "with really cool people."

And there's no doubt that *Retireat21,com* has delivered on those objectives for him. The formula is centered around interviews with top names in the online business, and Michael has been able to tap in to his father's extensive network of professionals to do this.

He really has interviewed some impressive names including:

- Darren Rowse
- Yaro Starak
- John Deiss
- Tony Hsieh
- Pete Cashmore
- Leo Babauta
- Jonathan Volk
- Gary Vaynerchuk

Indeed, the website has become the place to go when seeking information about any top names. Although the focus is on young entrepreneurs, it's drawing growing traffic from the older sector, who perhaps arrive to read an interview and then decide to stay around and find out more.

There's no doubt that he has used his father's contacts to his advantage – traveling with him to major online events around the world. But that's not to detract from his ability to get the big interviews with the players, while he's there. The interviews aren't formulaic either, he asks, and gets answered, some detailed and interesting questions.

On top of the interviews, he posts carefully designed content which is there to help aspiring Internet marketers and bloggers. Website tutorials, articles about different ways to make money online, and a series of "lists" which have generated a huge amount of traffic. You'll find an Internet "rich list" on the site, a list of entrepreneurs who make their living online who are under 30, and a list of bloggers under 21 ranked according to their website's influence.

Behind the scenes there is an extremely active forum, with over 5,000 members and 11,000 posts. Michael has focused from the beginning on creating a community around his brand, and it's this strong community which provides him with his income.

Retireat21.com is quite heavily monetized, with a fair amount of direct advertising. But the bulk of Michael's income derives from affiliate programs. Potential young entrepreneurs are attracted to the site to find out how this young man has been so successful. They are then skillfully shown how they can do the same, with a step by step on how to create a successful blog. At each stage they are offered a series of alternatives in terms of hosting, themes, domains and blogging tools. Each goes to sales pages via affiliate links.

The content of the tutorials on blogging and affiliate marketing are top class – and they genuinely offer a wide choice, with each recommended product reviewed honestly. Potential clients aren't being shoehorned into the best paying product.

For those who don't work their way through the tutorials, there's an email capture form that leads to a well designed sales funnel. And of course, there's the forum area which provides lots of help and advice, as well as another opportunity to recommend affiliate products.

All in all, *Retireat21.com* is a smooth, well designed selling machine. It offers real value, but makes no secret of the fact that it's designed to do exactly what Michael set out to do – create a good online income, with the minimum of on-going work.

Part of Michael's continuing success is that he is passionate about helping young (and old!) bloggers, and he does take the time and trouble to interact on the forum and to answer emails. He's also active on Twitter.

One strength of Michael's strengths that helps him stand apart from many other bloggers is that he has been very good at generating offline publicity. His story, which is fascinating, has been covered in newspapers all around the world. And online, he has been able to create the same buzz by networking at all the major blogging and online events, often travelling a long way to do so.

Spinning out of *Retireat21.com*, his most recent site, Incomediary.com has pushed even further into similar areas. The site is centered around sharing the enviable lifestyle Michael has created with his online endeavors, and then showing people how to do the same, offering a free seven day course in how to get online and start earning money. Once again, the income is based on affiliate products, so the formula is similar.

One thing that consistently comes across in his sites and in interviews is his message that people really should take some action. He believes there's a huge group of people that are interested in, and want to make a living online, but who are caught in a mire of procrastination. He feels helping to kick start these people is one of his life's missions.

His is an impressive story. Despite dropping out of college, he has not only carved out a great business in a narrow niche, but he has also travelled all over the world, created a strong brand and online presence, given some excellent speeches at various events, and is genuinely living the oft spoken about "Internet lifestyle."

Michael Dunlop is very different to most of the other bloggers featured in this book, but it's that difference that makes him interesting. He's much younger than most bloggers, he would be the first to admit he isn't a great writer and his whole business plan is based on not having to work too many hours. He certainly leans more towards Internet marketing than blogging in the true sense.

However, he has used his blog to build a platform and it's one of the slickest affiliate sales sites I've seen, offering a good balance between content and sales pitches. I think we can all learn from this young man, and from his assertion that the start of the 21st century will always be remembered as the first decade of the young entrepreneur.

Career Renegade

As an entrepreneur, it's important that you think with the long term game in mind

Career Renegade

Jonathan Fields

There are a lot of misconceptions about what it takes to become a successful blogger and furthermore, what a blog should be used for. When most people think about popular blogs, they think of advertisements and eBooks, but there's another model that we believe is just as valuable if not more practical for the long term.

What we're talking about here is the model of using your blog as a platform...a sort of launching pad for a variety of projects so that you don't have to stick to a single business or monetization model. Someone that has pulled this off in an extraordinary way is the "[Career Renegade](#)" himself, Jonathan Fields.

Escaping the Job Trap

Jonathan actually began his career as a high profile lawyer earning over six figures per year. However, after years of working tirelessly in a high stress environment, his body gave way and he had to be hospitalized for a perforated intestine. Seeing this as a wakeup call, Jonathan recovered and then took the opportunity to change his life for the better.

He left his job as an attorney and took time off to learn the ropes of what it would take to become a personal trainer. Taking a job as a $12/hour assistant, he spent 18 months gaining experience and building his own personal training business, which launched successfully and helped him get back to his previous earning level.

Once he realized he could build businesses at will, he sold the personal training business and created another – this time a new age yoga studio that again became an overnight success.

When he'd had his fill of this one, he again sold it to new investors. This allowed him to take a year off to write his book, *Career Renegade*, which eventually became an Amazon Best Seller.

Although the early part of his career is proof that it is possible to create a successful business based on something you are passionate about, the book deal didn't come quite as easily as you would expect. In fact, Jonathan actually had to fight hard in order to launch it successfully.

The Tribal Author

On his new website, The Tribal Author, Jonathan speaks of how his publisher called him shortly before printing to mention that they were going to print far fewer books than they had initially planned.

Career Renegade

Their rationale was that the book industry was hurting and that they wanted to play it safe. However, Jonathan knew that the number of books printed initially would be crucial to the success of *Career Renegade*, so he brainstormed on how he could use his blog to sell more copies. The problem though, was that no one had heard of him yet, so he needed a way to launch a blog almost overnight.

To do this, Jonathan created a free manifesto, called *The Firefly Manifesto*, and launched it on his blog. He didn't ask for an email and instead asked that people share it with as many people as they could. *The Firefly Manifesto* shared Jonathan's story and explained how people could quit becoming "repeat job offenders." At the very end of the report, he linked to his book pre-order page and simply asked those that wanted to learn more to pre-order his book.

The manifesto was a huge success, went viral, and convinced his publisher to increase their initial numbers. The rest of the story is history, as *Career Renegade* became a hit and launched Jonathan to the top of the charts.

At that point, Jonathan had already launched and sold two successful businesses, had written a best seller, and now had a large blog following that was begging for more. Although Jonathan could have easily kicked back and spent the rest of his days sipping cocktails in Tahiti, he used his budding popularity to launch a speaking, consulting, and coaching service for fellow renegades.

He also just launched a new blog for self-publishers, called the *Tribal Author*, which employs a content strategy for tapping in to an entirely new audience. He has already created and filled his first *Tribal Author Camp* in New York, and seems poised to take the self-publishing world by storm.

The Trampoline Effect

One of the things we'll talk about in the 2nd half of *Beyond Blogging* is how to use your story as a launching pad for bigger and better things. As an entrepreneur, it's important that you think with the long term game in mind, and that's what Jonathan has done here. He launched a series of interviews called the *Renegade Profiles*, which were profiles of up and coming game changers and innovators. He also created a series of Renegade boot camps, which are a very cool way of taking people out of their element and creating a life changing experience so that essentially, they will come back to the real world with a passion for finally breaking the patterns that bind them to unhappiness.

Using what he calls, "A Brand of One," Jonathan has spent the latter portion of his career teaching people how to build a personal brand that helps them transform their life and create a living around their passion. He admits that there are some things that people just don't want to buy, which is where the challenge of finding a proper monetization strategy comes in to play. However, as he has proven with many of his business strategies, the trick is not in finding the right passion, but instead finding out how you can tap into the needs of others in order to create a successful business.

Jonathan's strategy essentially boils down to the following four steps:
1. Spend the time it takes to learn the ropes in whatever industry inspires you.
2. Study the industry to see which gaps exist in the market.
3. Learn how you can tap into the exclusive and higher priced market in that industry.
4. Combine the gaps with what makes you unique and launch your business around that.

Jonathan's fitness club, called **Sedona**, was basically a themed gym with educated personal training professionals. During his time as a personal trainer, making 12 bucks an hour, he learned that most of the people in this industry made a terrible living. So, rather than follow the traditional approach to fitness and personal training, he found a way that he could tap into the upper levels of that market so that he could charge more for the same service. This is really a lesson in business more than anything, as it only makes sense to go where the higher paying customers are.

Jonathan also knew that most fitness clubs scared people, which is why he created an environment that welcomed people rather than scared them away. Using his personal approach to fitness, he created a new business that made more money in its first month than many fitness clubs make in an entire year.

He repeated this approach with his yoga studio, **Sonic Yoga NYC**, which made yoga more accessible for those that wanted to try but were scared away by the subtleties of most yoga studios. Again, this business was a huge success because it broke the traditional barriers of what a yoga studio should look and feel like.

If you can't tell by now, Jonathan's strategy, which is brilliant, has been to take a passion, make it accessible, and charge more for it. By making each of his studios exclusive and unique, Jonathan found a way to earn a very nice living doing what others normally get paid peanuts for. It has worked for both the personal training and yoga studios, but also works with his consulting and boot camps. Because he taps into a different audience, he can charge a premium for his services.

The Importance of Personal Branding

What Jonathan learned through this process was that he could amplify his current potential by creating a personal brand around his accomplishments. Although he will be the first to admit that he should have started branding himself sooner, he was smart enough to capitalize on his success early by writing a book and launching a speaking and consulting career. The blog was crucial for this, as most people outside of his circle would not have known about him otherwise.

Using his manifesto, his **Renegade Profile** interviews, and his blog, he has been able to capture an entirely new audience that is eager and willing to learn from the renegade master. I want to make it clear though, that in Jonathan's case, the blog was much more of a marketing platform than a content portal.

This is the strategy that works for many entrepreneurs that aren't interested in writing for a living, but instead want to find a way to engage in speaking and consulting opportunities. It can also operate as a creative launching pad, from which new ventures can be formed. The power in having a platform of that magnitude is that you will attract JV partners willing to pay for your expertise, and more importantly, you can carry the success of one venture over to the next. Without a personal brand, or in this case a blog, it would be very difficult to maintain momentum from one business platform to the next. However, using a blog in this manner creates an umbrella from which any business can become successful. Virtually everything that Jonathan touches these days turns to gold, which is the effect of a powerful personal brand that encourages success.

The Problogger Himself

The secret to a successful blog is great content, and plenty of it

The Problogger Himself

Darren Rowse

Darren Rowse may be the most well known of the so called A-List bloggers. He's achieved that by simply producing a steady and constant stream of stunningly useful content on his aptly named site Problogger. There can hardly be a blogger in the world who hasn't at some time stumbled across advice from Darren, when searching for help on the craft.

And yet he started almost by accident! His story is fascinating:

Darren first came across blogging back in 2002, when he was working part time at three "normal" jobs. He was a minister specializing in helping young people in his local church, he was working in a warehouse for an online store, and he was a casual laborer taking on all kinds of jobs through a local temp agency. It was from these humble beginnings that the quintessential "Problogger" came and took the online world by storm.

Darren's first blog was a **Blogspot** special, where he simply recorded his thoughts and views, in common with many early bloggers, who were using the new medium as a kind of online diary. This continued for a year, at which point he set up a second blog related to his photography hobby. It was called *Digital Photography Blog(DPB)*.

While setting up *DPB*, Darren discovered both *AdSense*, and the *Amazon* affiliate program. Applying them to his new site, he hoped to at least offset the hosting costs.

Despite having a decent readership on both blogs, the income wasn't huge, slowly breaking through the dollar a day barrier, before moving to around $3 a day towards the end of his second year. Not a fantastic result, but more than enough to cover his costs.

At around this time, some decisions about the future had to be made. And in discussions with his wife V, Darren decided that he could realistically replace one of his part time jobs with blogging for an income. Whenever Darren writes about this period, he is at pains to point out that it was a tough decision, and that it took some considerable time, and a lot of post writing, to get to the point where he could even consider it.

Throughout 2004, Darren put two days a week (and a lot of late nights!) into his blogging. He was delighted to see earnings increase to the point where he seriously began to think about blogging as a long term career.

It's interesting to note that, in common with many bloggers, he went through several experimental stages, running up to 20 different blogs, in different niches, to try to find new revenue sources. He finally realized that he would be better off focusing on two or three key areas, so he bought the domain Problogger.net to allow him to share his tips about blogging. Combined with what had become Digital Photography School (DPS, formerly DPB), he now had two core blogs from which to expand his empire.

Darren will tell you over and over again that the secret to a successful blog is great content, and plenty of it. True to form, he posted over 1800 times on Problogger in the first 15 months of it's life. I'll save you the math - that's an **average** of 4 posts a day, every single day! During this period, he was regularly working into the small hours to build his burgeoning empire.

2005 was the seminal year for Darren - despite a hiccup at the start of the year, he effectively became a full time blogger. It's interesting to note the reactions of friends and family to this decision, as they often asked how his "hobby" was going and asked him when he was going to get a proper job! Despite that, the decision proved to be a wise one, and during the course of the year **DPS** and **Problogger** became hugely successful and finally brought him in a genuine full time salary.

Whilst he took the decision to concentrate on **Problogger** and **DPS**, he was still interested in other ventures, and this lead him to become a joint founder of **B5 Media**, a company that has grown to become a real blogging powerhouse, with a network of blogs enjoying over 10 million page views every month.

The last few years have seen Darren consolidate *DPS* to become one of the world's most read photography blogs, with *Problogger* emerging as the best site there is for new and learning bloggers. *DPS* makes huge revenues from advertising and from selling cameras and associated equipment through *Amazon,* while *Problogger* makes it's money through selling Darren's own products, affiliations, and the recently launched *Problogger.com* forum.

The newest addition to the stable has been *Twitip*, a site that focuses on helping readers to understand and get the best from the Twitter micro-blogging platform. Having been through a traffic growth phase, *Twitip* is now being monetized, with advertising being offered, as well as several Twitter related products being sold through the site.

Although he is patently a shy person, Darren has been extremely effective in using offline media to promote his various projects. He's been interviewed for Australian television and radio several times, he constantly appears in local and international press and is generally regarded in the media world as a "voice."

He's had two features in *The Wall Street Journal*, one in *Business Week*, which is a great indicator of the value of getting coverage in offline media, as each interview has brought him a significant number of new readers.

The Problogger Himself

An interesting trait that differentiates Darren from some bloggers is his desire to keep his personal life private. He occasionally refers to his wife, but only as "V" and we do know he has a son, but by and large he keeps that side of his life quiet.

In 2008, a publisher approached him and suggested a book about blogging for a living could be a big seller. Darren teamed up with Chris Garrett to produce *Problogger – Secrets for Blogging Your Way to a Six Figure* income. The book has become a big seller, and pulls together much of the learning from the posts Darren has written over the years, re-ordering it and bringing it up to date.

2009 saw Darren launch the incredible *31 Days to be a better blogger course* – which he offered completely free of charge, and which took approximately 12,000 people through the basic steps needed to create a blog.

This was an amazing example of giving away free content and instantly created a huge community of fans, many of whom have since joined the paid-for forum at *Problogger.com* At the end of the course participants were offered the chance to buy a workbook, and large numbers did so.

So where is he today?

The mad rush of posting and working until the small hours has eased off, although Darren admits he still sometimes puts too many hours in on his Mac!

1. *Problogger* now generates a substantial income through sales of the book, the *31 Days workbook*, the forum and through direct advertising. It remains the first stop for bloggers needing solid information about the subject. Darren remains the main writer for this blog, although he does run guest posts quite regularly.
2. *Digital Photography School* is simply huge, with massive traffic and a thriving vibrant community in the forum area. The income here comes via *AdSense*, direct advertising and fabulous use of the Amazon affiliate program to sell cameras and accessories. *DPS* has a team of writers, and Darren is a regular contributor to the site.
3. *Twitip* is still finding it's voice, but is establishing itself as the site for information about how to get the best from the new medium.
4. *B5 Media* is growing into a very large network of blogs and Darren enjoys his position as Director of Blogger Training.

Darren is not a typical entrepreneur. He's quiet, thoughtful and self-effacing. He's not a natural at self-promotion, and he isn't confident on camera or in public, but he makes up for those deficiencies with an awesome work ethic and a genuine desire to help people. For those of you who share those traits, he's an inspiration that you don't need to be an energized marketer to make it online.

The Problogger Himself

Summary and Key Points

- It took almost three years of extremely hard work for Darren to become a full time, professional blogger.
- The basis of his success has been in writing extraordinary amounts of content, which is incredibly helpful.
- He spends a great deal of energy in understanding his audience and what they need from him.
- He has learned that he is more effective in focusing on a few key projects rather than spreading himself across many.
- Darren has made good use of offline media's fascination with the subject of blogging and earning an income online.
- He has consistently avoided the "Big ticket" course or membership program as a means of earning money, instead focusing on leveraging his large audience to buy inexpensive, good value for money products.
- He elicited the support of his wife at every stage of his blogging career, never jeopardizing that relationship by taking risks.

Video Star

She's essentially perfected the art of viral video... full transparency is a large part of what helped her capture the hearts of her fans

Video Star

iJustine

A lot of traditional blogging advice is geared for written blogs, but the truth is that there are many video blogs that are not only more popular than print blogs, but that also create bigger stars. One of these stars, and perhaps an Internet meme all to herself (in fact, she dubs herself "the Internet") is iJustine, who became famous making viral videos before the term was commonplace.

iJustine, and most vlogging stars as a whole, make very interesting case studies because it can be difficult to pinpoint what it is they do that makes them stand out. Sure, they make cool videos, but video content is typically difficult to monetize, which means that vloggers have to be forward thinking and stay ahead in the monetization game. They are often tech geeks and remarkably clever PR types. Justine (her full name is Justine Ezarik) is certainly one of these people, as she fancies herself an Apple fan girl and a technology freak, but her uniqueness doesn't stop there.

iJustine has figured out how to capitalize on every inch of Internet fame that she's garnered, turning it into over 800 thousand YouTube subscribers, over 700 thousand Twitter followers, and a career that is skyrocketing. She recently earned a spot at the MTV VMA's as the

Twitter correspondent, has signed on to Carson Daly's new *"The Really Big Internet Show,"* and has frequently been featured as a speaker at popular blogging conferences and tech shows.

Perhaps the most exciting story here though, is not that iJustine has capitalized on her Internet fame, but the manner in which she became famous in the first place. You would think that it takes perfect content and a great group of fans to help you became famous as a video blogger, but iJustine's story proves that isn't the case.

iJustine actually started as a life-streamer, which she did by creating a funky hat camera and filming her every move. She kept the broadcast live, 24/7, and was not shy about meeting people, many of them Internet stalkers. As her popularity began to grow, she started getting offers to cover specific products, which led to her being hired by **Technology Evangelist**, a popular technology blog, to cover the Apple iPhone release in the **Mall of America**. From there, she ended up with her own iPhone, which is where her popularity really started to take off.

Justine created a short video, called "My 300 page iPhone Bill," which featured a page turning account of her first bill from AT&T, which arrived in a box and provided a detailed account of every call, text, and download onto her new phone. The video was made in 2007, and has since received over 2 million views

Video Star

on YouTube alone. The video went viral, and received such a large outpouring of comments that AT&T actually changed their billing format shortly after.

From there, iJustine's popularity skyrocketed, and she capitalized by becoming a permanent vlogger and YouTube star. These days, she creates a variety of parody videos based on Internet memes and trendy entertainment topics. She does a brilliant job of leveraging pop-culture and meshing it with her technology background, creating hilariously catchy videos.

Breaking down the details of Justine's rise to fame, there are quite a few interesting points to note. For one, although there were many people doing the same thing at the time, there were a few things that Justine had going for her that others didn't.

For starters, let's be honest…she is a young and attractive woman, which means that she was a perfect fit for the teenage demographic that is often found on sites like YouTube. She also is extremely and unabashedly outgoing, which made it easy for her to interact and engage with her public. As her audience grew, she would give them opportunities to see her in public, whether at the coffee shop, at restaurants, or while travelling. Lastly, unlike many other life-streamers, she wasn't afraid to show it all (aside from private moments). The transparency here is an important point, one which we will discuss at length in the upcoming chapters.

Once she gave up life-streaming, she was smart enough to know how to keep her audience growing even as her medium changed. Although her videos would have you believe that she's just a ditzy blonde, the truth is that she is technologically savvy and knows how to make videos that look good. She's essentially perfected the art of viral video, and has used her popularity as a springboard for consulting and speaking deals. With Justine, there is certainly "more than meets the eye."

Traffic

Where many bloggers might excel at making online connections and using strategies like commenting and guest posts to leverage communities, Justine made live connections to develop a devoted fan base that followed her every move. Sure, you could say she risked personal safety and privacy in her efforts to get noticed, but the truth is that it worked!

iJustine keeps her finger on the pulse of the Internet and entertainment industries so that she is able to either poke fun of them in a parody video or bring you a firsthand perspective via a behind the scenes video. This is how she mastered the art of viral videos and has been able to consistently increase her online presence. She's been able to be a first responder on YouTube, which means that her videos are often instant hits, but it comes at a price. She has to be insanely quick on the draw, meaning that she has to be able to crank out videos on the fly as the news breaks. However, she's obviously proven that she can not only make quick videos, but that she can make entertaining videos that are well produced and original.

In the beginning of her career, when she took the leap of faith to go from graphic design to life-streaming, she made sure to dive in 100%. Her willingness to be completely authentic and allow for full transparency is a large part of what helped her capture the hearts of her fans. She wasn't afraid to connect either, which had her fans glued to the computer screen in the hopes of being able to find her out in public. This is the same sort of presence that guys like Chris Brogan and Gary Vaynerchuk maintain, as people are always on the lookout for them at blogging events and conferences. The important thing to highlight here is that as an Internet personality, if you hide behind your camera, you are going to be labeled a fraud. In creating live connections with her fans, Justine kept fueling the viral engine that helped her explode onto the scene.

Content

iJustine doesn't really offer anything you couldn't live without. Yeah, her videos are catchy and hilarious, but they are also forgettable, which means that she is in the unfortunate situation of always chasing the next hit. She doesn't let this faze her though, because she's following her passion and seems driven to create content whether or not she's getting paid. She loves what she's doing, and it shows.

She is also smart enough to know how to leverage communities, and she'll often create contests or challenge her audience to help her achieve goals, like appearing on *The Ellen Show.* The key here is that in enlisting the aid of her audience, she is bringing them along with her and creating her own "Tribe," a term coined by Seth Godin.

What makes Justine's content stand out is not that it is remarkable, but that it is consistent and focused on popular topics. She knows her demographic and as such, she can churn out content that they'll keep coming back for.

Monetization

As we've said before, video content can be very difficult to monetize in a manner that is not obtrusive to the content. The options of sponsored videos are always there, but people like Justine need to remember to keep the audience first and cannot afford to sacrifice their credibility to make a buck. Although I can't say for sure which products she's been paid to endorse, looking through her blog you can make a guess at a few. For instance, some of her posts on Apple products are more promotional than her normal posts, as are the posts in which she recommends photographers, and specific social networking services.

Like many other popular YouTube personalities, Justine makes money from video views a well. The model that YouTube uses is the CPM model, which generally pays a set amount for every 1,000 views. Although some reports have shown the Google owned YouTube paying up to $20 per thousand views, more realistic estimates show an average of around $1 for every thousand views. This means that a video with 1 million hits can expect to see a return of only $1,000, which means that you either need to create a massively successful video or a string of mildly popular ones in order to make even a small living from this model.

Lastly, and probably the most effective method of monetization for Justine, is the offline method, which allows her to monetize her expertise by offering consulting services and speaking engagements. Although this method requires her to trade hours for dollars, her unique position allows her to charge a premium for that time. As her popularity continues to grow and the traditional media types learn about her, I expect that she'll be pitched for more than just

Internet TV shows and her guest spot at the VMA's will prove to be small time compared to what lies ahead.

Although Justine has stated publicly that she is not a fan of many Internet to TV moves, if her recent spot on MTV is any indication, she seems to do well in the spotlight.

Video Star

The Original Personal Development Blogger

Steve Pavlina once again proves that there is no single "formula" for success online

The Original Personal Development Blogger

Steve Pavlina

Steve Pavlina is one of the world's most successful personal development bloggers, and is hugely influential in those circles, with perhaps the largest blog of all in that niche – the site enjoys over 2 million monthly readers. He's also a successful author and public speaker and he carries out a series of personal development workshops.

The journey really began for him when he was arrested for theft. He found himself languishing in a jail cell at the age of 19. Realizing he was seeing the pattern for his future life, he decided it was time to change things, and since then he has lived and breathed personal development, often experimenting on himself for the benefit of his readers.

He went on to earn degrees in mathematics and computer science and then founded a business in the computer games industry. But it wasn't until he decided to share his passion for his own personal growth through the blog, that he really found his way in life.

His experiments with polyphasic sleeping are an example of his commitment to his craft. For five months he slept for just two hours a day, documenting the results on his blog. He also switched first to a vegan diet, and more recently to a purely raw food diet.

Once again, he has been candid about the effects, both positive and negative. At times it can seem as though Steve is constantly searching for new experiences and new stuff to try, and that is one of the facets that makes the blog such a compelling read.

It's this level of commitment that has allowed him to build huge authority in the niche and the blog has grown consequentially. Nowadays, the blog does not focus at all on what we would call traditional community building or monetization techniques, although it once did.

When he started the StevePavlina.com in October 2004, his focus was on traffic building, and this was done simply by writing great free content for the site. It worked! Within 18 months he was generating over a million visitors per month, which is extraordinary growth. His monetization strategy was simple – he had six strands:

- *Google AdSense*
- Donations
- Sold text link adverts
- *Chitika* mini malls
- *Amazon* affiliate links
- Static advertising sold to individual advertisers

Within two years, these strands were bringing in over $1000 a day. A thriving community had built up around the blog, with over 100 comments being added to many posts.

The Original Personal Development Blogger

All in all, he was a stunning success story – creating a blog that went from nowhere to mainstream, with a massive income, in a little over two years. So Steve, typically, decided to change everything!

In two dramatic moves, he removed all third-party advertising from the site and closed blog comments.

At the time he stopped advertising, he was earning over $100,000 a year from *AdSense* alone. So why did he do it? The two main reasons he cites are that the advertising being served wasn't matching his ideas and ideals for the blog, and that he felt that *"sucking at the teat"* of advertising was making life too easy, and he wanted more challenges.

On the closing of comments, he said felt too much of his time was being taken up dealing with them and all the attendant spam, and that the vast majority of his readers were neither making nor reading the comments on most blog posts.

If you follow conventional wisdom, closing comments should have killed his blog. It didn't and it remains firmly in *Alexa's* top 10,000 websites in the world.

These days, Steve's considerable income derives from offering some carefully picked affiliate products via the site, as well as selling his own books and his *Conscious Growth* workshops.

His brand has grown with his authority and he is now a world recognized figure in the raw food movement, as well as a member of the *Transformational Leadership Council.*

Steve's writing style is also quite different to many bloggers. He updates without recourse to a schedule, so posts appear when they are ready. They are much longer than most blogger's posts, often 2000 to 3000 words, and one that I recently read was over 7000 words long! He likes to explore each subject in great detail.

His writing on traditional personal development ideas can be inspiring – he talks from a common sense viewpoint, and as pointed out earlier, practices what he preaches. But he can also be "edgy." During 2009, he wrote about his interest in polyamory (having several loving relationships) and his plan to develop himself with polyamory in mind. At the time his wife Erin was supportive of the idea, but it came as little surprise to readers when he later announced their separation on the blog. He and Erin remain good friends, and Steve continues to be a great supporter of her blog and business.

Typically, Steve hasn't adapted to Twitter in the way that many bloggers have. He's an infrequent user of the medium and has built up a relatively small following and follows few people himself.

In fact, he does seem slow to adopt to new aspects of social media – only recently has he started video blogging, and his video blogs aren't quite there yet, following the long prose style of his writing. He does Podcast and has a very successful audio series available for download.

The Original Personal Development Blogger

It's interesting trawling through the archives on Steve's blog. As you would expect, they accurately reflect his change and growth. Many of the early pieces focus on almost traditional "How to" strategies for bloggers, sharing his success and ideas for generating traffic and earning more income from advertising. Once he had achieved that, he then moved into more normal personal development areas like self-discipline, defining a life purpose and life improvement material. Recently he has moved into more spiritual areas, covering religion and a great deal of relationship material. He has managed to keep each segment of readers along the way as his blog and direction have changed.

Steve Pavlina once again proves that there is no single "formula" for success online. In many ways he has done the opposite to the advice given by most bloggers. He doesn't actively cultivate a community around his blog, he often strays far outside his niche, and he has ditched the conventional advertising that was creating a huge passive income for him. He doesn't do guest posts on other blogs and he doesn't allow others to guest on his blog, and he won't consider an interview with any other blogger unless they can demonstrate an audience of 50,000 or more readers. And yet despite all this, he remains at the top of his game, constantly surprising readers, and continuing to make a solid income based around his blog.

The Real Man behind the Curtain

Proof that if you master basic business skills, combine them with Internet Marketing skills, and blog without throwing away your integrity, then you will be capable of virtually anything

The Real Man behind the Curtain

Brian Clark

Perhaps no blogger is more mysterious than the man behind the curtain of Copyblogger, Brian Clark. It's not that he doesn't post (he does), or that he avoids public appearances (he speaks at a handful of conferences each year), it's just that his monetization models are more discreet than those of other bloggers featured in this volume.

For instance, there are whispers of income as high as $100k/month and *Copyblogger* revenue of over 3 million in 2009 alone, but to the average blogger, there's no evidence of where the money comes from. On the surface, *Copyblogger* doesn't sell anything at all. Sure, they review and promote affiliate products from time to time, but not to the tune of a 7 figure business.

Outside of *Copyblogger*, it's tough to find Brian involved in anything else, which begs the question, what is he really doing, and how can we learn to do it? Well, to get to the heart of that question, we'll have to step back to years before Copyblogger was founded and to the time that Brian was still working as a lawyer. Although Brian was a successful lawyer, like many other overworked professionals, he was burned out and looking for a new way to do business.

How an Attorney Changes the Face of Blogging

Intrigued by the Internet, Brian made use of his marketing and legal expertise to launch an incredibly successful online Real Estate brokerage firm. If you dig hard enough, you'll find that he did this using a single white paper that gave the secrets to the MLS, which is the backbone of the Real Estate industry; a textbook case of using free information to recruit a devoted following.

From there, Brian worked the Internet Marketing circles, at one point helping an ACH (the bank payment system) firm bring in a total of 100k per month, 40k of which he got to keep. Eventually though, he got the call to do something different, which is when ***Copyblogger*** was born.

When he formed ***Copyblogger*** in January of 2006, Brian had a burning desire to prove that Internet marketing tactics could also work for bloggers. He'd already learned how to sell high value information and earn a healthy living in the process, but with ***Copyblogger,*** he couldn't just come in and start asking customers to hand over their wallet.

At the time, selling products from blogs was unheard of, which meant that Brian had to give consistently for over a year before he would think about monetizing. So Brian posted new content every single day on ***Copyblogger***; teaching bloggers how to write better copy for their websites and sales pages. If you look through the post archives, you'll see some of the A-list rockstars, who at the time were

The Real Man behind the Curtain

unknown, hanging out in the comments section. Guys like Chris Brogan, Chris Garrett, Chris Pirillo, and gals like Liz Strauss were just beginning their ascent to success at the time.

Eventually, Brian used his growing readership and authority presence to launch a course called *Teaching Sells*, which taught bloggers how to make money by teaching, rather than selling. He's launched it twice more since then, each time bringing in more profit that the last. In fact, the last launch of *Teaching Sells* sold 500 seats, at a price of roughly $2,000, in just one day. In an interview, Brian mentioned that the total sales (after refunds, bounced cards, etc) was around $800,000. And that was the second time it had launched in 2009.

Outside of *Teaching Sells*, Brian also co-founded the *Thesis Theme for WordPress* with developer Chris Pearson, which has since become the most popular *WordPress* theme on the planet. At well over 2 million dollars in sales, Thesis no doubt accounts for a large portion of *Copyblogger's* revenue.

Coming soon, Brian, Sonia Simone (Senior Editor at *Copyblogger*), Darren Rowse, and Chris Brogan will be launching a new product, called *Internet Marketing for Smart People.* The details at this point are hush-hush, but you can expect that with those names involved, it's going to be big, if not bigger than anything done in the niche before.

Brian's Million Dollar Formula

Brian is a legend, and there's good reason for it. But, there is no reason why you cannot become a legend in your own right. The tactics that Brian used to scale the face of the blogging world will work in any niche and with any style of blog. It might be hard to believe, but the only difference between you and Brian is time.

Step 1: Deliver content like crazy

Copyblogger's formula is to deliver content on a daily basis (M-F) that provides tremendous value to the reader. Call it cookie content (Sonia's term for teaching readers to come back for more), call it juicy content, call it whatever you like. You've got to have great content that you can deliver as often as you have time for and in a manner that is consistent with how your audience seeks to consume it.

Step 2: Free Reports

There's a post on *Copyblogger* that shows how Brian was able to help a blog go from 0 to over 6,000 feed subscribers in a single day, all using a free PDF report. He used the same strategy to launch *Teaching Sell*s, and to help *Copyblogger* reach an audience of over 70k subscribers.

His free reports aren't just run of the mill information though. He uses them to give away some of his secrets, knowing that those secrets will be the hook that snares the reader into wanting more. His reports usually don't require an email address, which makes it even easier to spread them throughout the web.

Step 3: Team with Rockstars

Brian isn't a theme developer, but he knows what a blogger wants in a theme. He's also a remarkably underrated businessman, which is how he was able to work with Chris to create a theme that rocked the blogging world. *Thesis* is now used by some of the most powerful names in the blogging world, and thanks to a number of affiliate partnerships, Thesis has very little competition.

Brian is also smart enough to know that being stuck behind the desk at *Copyblogger* could only stifle other, more productive, projects. This is why he recruited Sonia (who is amazing in her own right) and often recruits guest posts from other bloggers. This frees him up to think ahead, a task that many bloggers do not have time for.

The Sacred Art of Combining Internet Marketing with Integrity

This is, in my opinion, Brian's greatest accomplishment to date. He's managed to find a way to combine Internet Marketing with blogging in a way that isn't seedy or corrupt. He's taken the best of both worlds and learned how to create products that help people.

Using his knowledge and expertise, he could easily have made a fortune by selling dreams to the ignorant, but instead he's found a way to make Internet Marketing fun and easy. Part of the way he does this is by being choosy with the products that he promotes as an affiliate, but the rest lies in the fact that he's been giving away information for 4 years now. He's trusted, and because of that, he has an authority presence that few have been able to achieve.

Brian is the prototype for a new, evolved, blogger. He's proof that if you master basic business skills, combine them with Internet Marketing skills, and blog without throwing away your integrity, then you will be capable of virtually anything. Don't confuse that with being afraid to make a buck though, because Brian will tell you he has no problem charging a premium for information products and using traditional launch tactics. The difference between him and others though, is that he delivers on his promise.

If you are looking for a business model to take you Beyond Blogging, then Brian Clark might be the best example we can provide. You might have to deliver free content for a year or more before you reach the level of success that you desire, but if you simply master the basics mentioned here, then you will be far ahead of most.

The Real Man behind the Curtain

The Six Figure Blogging Blueprint

The Six Figure Blogging Blueprint

Find your passion

One thing all the bloggers in this book have in common is a passion for what they do. Sure, it varies in intensity – at one end of the scale we have Gary Vaynerchuk who bleeds passion from every pore, and at the other Darren Rowse, who is often shy and reticent. But don't mistake that for a lack of passion, his passion just manifests itself differently.

And they each have a deep seated motivation, which once again varies from blogger to blogger – for some it's the money, pure and simple. For others security, fame, and a feeling of success.

Combining motivation and passion leads us to that "certain something" that differentiates "our" bloggers from the common herd - the often intangible asset that allowed them to rise up through the primordial soup of thousands of people all talking about the same thing, at the same time.

Make no mistake, each of our stars has something that triggered that asset within them, and when they discovered what is was, they simply had to tap into it consistently.

So what does all this mean for you and for me? As a first step, we need to find a niche that will drive a passion within us for the long term. Something that will maintain our own interest and drive for years. For Gary, it was wine, although it could equally have been the New York Jets. For Chris Brogan it was social media itself.

For Chris Garrett and Darren Rowse it was about helping other bloggers to succeed.

So what's your passion? How do you find it? Here are some questions which may help:
- What animates you, gets you excited?
- What do you know a lot about?
- What do you enjoy studying or reading about?
- What do you do a lot of in your spare time?

And here's the best test. Imagine you are about to land a job as a blogger. You're going to be paid a salary of $100,000 a year, with the only stipulation being that you have to write 5 posts a week. You can choose any topic you want for the blog. Don't pause to think about it. What's the topic going to be? Having established a topic we can be passionate about, the next hurdle is to become overtly passionate on the subject. The problem we all face these days is that it's not actually "cool" to be passionate or animated, and this is something we all really have to overcome. In that sense blogging is a little like acting – our gestures, our words, our thoughts, our points of view have to be bigger, even slightly exaggerated, to gain credence on the big stage.

Next we need to find a way to create our motivation, and this is all about working towards goals and objectives. In this area, our findings were unanimous. Every one of the bloggers featured in **Beyond Blogging** has clearly defined goals for their businesses, from long term goals, to daily objectives and task lists. And they all agreed that these goals provided the motivation to keep them going and to keep achieving.

Finally in this section, we need to talk about finding our distinguishing factor. And this is perhaps the hardest thing of all. It's not even something we can help you with – it has to come from within yourself, but it is there.

There is something unique, something special that you can bring to whatever niche you choose to enter. And you need to discover it and exploit it if you truly want to join the ranks of the blogging superstars.

Building a Platform

So you've got a niche, you've identified your passion, and you are excited about creating a business. That's the fun part, and it's important because the energy from that passion will be the gas tank that fuels the rest of your journey. If you haven't identified that passion correctly, you'll know it sooner than later because in the future, when it's time to burn that midnight oil, you won't have any left to burn.

In observing our list of bloggers, it's clear that in order to establish a clear and authoritative online identity, you've got to have a platform from which to launch not only products, but ideas and opinions as well. It is from this platform that you will find which ideas your audience bonds to, what they are looking for in a leader of your type, and how you can best serve them.

This platform generally revolves around a blog, but there's so much more to it than just posting new content a few times per week. Building a platform, building a blog even, is like building any other business…you have to plan carefully and be methodical in your approach. There are specific details that cannot be ignored, and specific steps that need to be followed. We're going to talk about those next.

Design

I mention design first for several reasons, but primarily because if you are going to build a professional platform, then you are going to have to make sure that the look and feel of your blog matches that theme. These days, it's simply not good enough to download a free **WordPress** theme and expect it to work…not if you are building a business.

Sure, free themes work great for small niche sites that are **AdSense** driven, but not so much with business platforms. And you'll notice that I'm beating this term, platform, into your head, because your blog is the pulpit from which you preach. If it looks like garbage, then you'll have a hard time building an audience, no matter how great the content might be.

So when you start shopping for themes, find one that is either rarely used or buy a theme like the Thesis or Headway Theme and have it customized, which you can do for around $500-$1000. It might sound like a lot of money, especially when you've been told that you can start a blog on a shoestring, but it might be the most important $500 you'll ever spend.

Why now, you ask? Why not start free and move to a more expensive theme when your blog takes off? Because of first impressions.

Think about the number of visitors you'll need to have created a successful blog. The number is probably in the thousands. Now, picture those visitors as customers, and your blog as a shopping mall. Imagine that instead of walking into a well-established, impressively designed structure, they walk in to see bare walls with nothing but drywall…no paint, and stores without signs, branding, or price tags.

How many of those shoppers do you think would walk in, take a look, and then walk right out? Not only will most of them be turned off by the appearance of that mall and exit the minute they arrive, but they'll also go home and tell their friends that your mall sucks. Those friends will have an impression of that mall, without ever stepping foot inside of it. So you are already down 2 levels of influence, without any way to get them back. Because even if you do finish the paint and get the signs up, add pretty flowers, and wax the floors, they'll still remember your mall as the bare walled hole in the wall, that doesn't have anything to offer.

Think of all the effort you would have to spend to get those customers back in to your mall. Then imagine the effort of having to convince them to tell their friends that your mall isn't so bad after all. It would be a hell of a lot of work, right?

That's what you are dealing with when you avoid starting with a good blog design, only sometimes on an even grander scale thanks to mediums like Twitter, Facebook, Digg, Reddit, StumbleUpon, and YouTube. Instead of having to waste effort down the road trying to chase customers, why not wow them right off the bat? 9 times out of 10, they won't check your subscriber counts, they won't go to *Compete.com* and check your traffic, and they won't check your Alexa ranking. If they show up to a kick ass neighborhood and drive up to a beautiful house, they will automatically assume that you've got it going on. That's why design matters, and that's why you can't wait till later.

If you look at the websites of the bloggers in this guide, you'll see that almost all of them have paid to have custom themes built from scratch. Most of those that didn't use some form of the **Thesis Theme** and had it customized for their brand.

Sure, they might not have paid $2,000 for a theme right from the start, but all started with something uniquely special to their brand. Brian Clark, for instance, teamed up with rockstar developer Chris Pearson to create the **Copyblogger Theme**. Chris Guillebeau hired all star designer, Reese Spykerman, right off the bat. He even hired a photographer to take professional pictures so that he could make an even greater impression for those critical first visitors.

Each of these bloggers understood the importance of building a brand around their platform, and they went out and hired the best designer they could afford. The results are in – it worked.

So don't skimp on design, even if you have to spend more than makes you comfortable. We're not saying you should mortgage your home to get it done, but think of other ways that you can raise the money, such as freelance work, bartering, or selling stuff on eBay. If you think about your skills and the assets you have to raise money, then surely there is a way that you can come up with a few hundred bucks. If you can't, then just keep saving.

Branding

We talked about branding a bit in the previous chapter, but I wanted to touch on it one more time because it's really important. Branding isn't just a logo, or a banner on your blog. It's the font you use, the graphics you use, the color of your background, the texture, the look, smell, taste, and feel of your platform.

Your brand should be echoed in everything you say, meaning that if you jump around and have difficulty staying on topic, then your message will be lost on your readers. Each of the featured bloggers in our story has chosen a specific theme to represent:

- Chris Guillebeau: Non-Conformity
- Brian Clark: Copywriting for Bloggers
- Gary Vaynerchuk: Making Wine Easy
- Chris Brogan: The Human Side of New Media
- Jonathan Fields: Career Renegade

As you can see, each blogger has narrowed down their niche and used their content to drill that image into the minds of their readers. Everything that Chris Guillebeau writes about has to do with living an unconventional life. Everything that David Risely does echoes his experience as a six-figure blogger.

If you don't identify a unique brand that not only helps you stand out, but identifies how you can help your readers, then you are going to struggle. So spend some time thinking about what makes you tick, how your knowledge and expertise can benefit your readers, and how you can wrap it all up in one pretty package.

The End Benefits

Let's halt the talk on branding and design for a minute, and look behind the curtain, so to speak. Notice that many of these bloggers do not monetize directly to their audience. Instead, their blog functions as a platform (there's that word again) that builds their personal brand.

It is this brand, as it is built over time, that allows them to earn money behind the scenes, which we'll talk about in a few chapters.

Don't think that you have to sell E-Books and consulting to create a successful blogging business. Think bigger than that. Think syndicated content (Penelope Trunk makes 5 figures per month by allowing other information outlets to syndicate her blog posts), think book deals, think blog network, and more. There are so many opportunities that will present themselves to those with a reputable platform, that most of them aren't even visible to the end user.

It's Field of Dreams baby – "If You Build It, They Will Come."

Building a Tribe

Building a platform is like building a store. You've got to have one before you place a sign in the window and start selling your brand and the products within that brand. However, just as with any other business, having a store doesn't guarantee an income… you need people to walk in the door and pull out their wallet.

A normal business does this by advertising in the Yellow Pages, newspaper, magazines, billboards, and now – social media, but how does a blog do it? How can you get people to not only visit your store, but to hang out, grab a coffee, and make it their 2nd home?

Well, the trick is not in convincing people to come over, but in recruiting them to your cause. You do this not by advertising your blog, but by building a tribe around your own personal brand.

One of the best at this is Chris Guillebeau, who built a massive audience that he calls, "A Small Army of Remarkable People." Jonathan Fields has a group of "Career Renegades" and Gary V has the "Vayner Nation," but the rest of the bloggers featured here have similarly devoted, albeit unnamed, fan clubs.

What makes these groups of people fans, more than customers, is that they are not only supporters of their leader, but they are fiercely devoted and act as brand evangelists – for free.

Although having 10,000 readers is great, having 1,000 fans is far more powerful. But the question remains then, how does one achieve this sort of loyal fan base. What are the steps to building a tribe that will rapidly consume every piece of content that you can create, and then share the crumbs with their friends?

We've analyzed the heck out of these A-Listers to find out, and came up with a three step process.

1. Become entrenched
2. Engage
3. Give it all away

Become Entrenched

The road to becoming respected in any niche starts with possessing that which is essential to being an authority, or in other words, knowledge. With knowledge comes both the understanding of how to speak to the people within that niche, and the battery of opinions that are required in order to craft compelling and insightful commentary.

Without content, which we'll talk about shortly, your blog lacks power. Every single blogger in this volume has amassed an impressive amount of knowledge for their respective niche.

Gary Vaynerchuk said that before he started selling wine, he invested himself into becoming a wine authority, which meant he had to learn not only the lingo, but the very essence of what makes wine people tick.

The wine niche, in particular, is one deeply routed in opinion and subjective taste. Had Gary not studied his chosen domain, he would have been quickly outed as an imposter. Had Chris Guillebeau not actually traveled around the world, or successfully created online businesses, his entire volume of essays would have been grounded in falsehoods.

Although old school brand professionals and PR types have called Chris Brogan an illusionist, the truth is that his beliefs are grounded in real world experience. Although he wasn't raised in PR, his ability to tackle the gatekeepers in that industry is a result of his passion for his niche and the willingness to dive in head first as a trailblazer.

Penelope Trunk practices what she preaches, Chris Garret built authority on several occasions, and David Risley built a six figure blogging business before he told people how to create one.

What we're trying to say here is that you can't blog about making money online if you haven't done it. You can't be the guy that reviews beers if you don't understand the processes involved in brewing them, or at a minimum, the differences in styles of beers.

Don't put the cart ahead of the horse and expect to skate by without doing your homework. That manner of doing business is a disservice to both yourself and your audience.

It is easy to rebuild fortunes, but reputations are much more difficult to repair. In building your business, remember that if you want to be a teacher, you have to receive an education first.

If you don't understand a niche, it doesn't mean you can't talk about it. For instance, many bloggers have become successful by adopting a "walk with me" method, whereby they take readers on a journey from start to finish.

The thing is, and we talked about it earlier, it is advisable not to follow the money, but to follow your passion. If passion is your guide, then you will never be energy poor, and it will show in your content.

Engage

This is the bread and butter of building a tribe. Engaging, not only with your community, but with those outside of your own, is the first key to building your own "Small Army."

Engaging isn't just answering comments and replying to emails. It isn't just RT'ing and replying on Twitter in hopes of getting reciprocal backlinks.

It's not complex, but it is difficult, because it requires an investment of time and energy that many bloggers are not willing to make.

In the beginning, it's just you. You might have made a reader out of your mom, dad, grandma, grandpa, husband, or wife, but outside of that things look pretty thin.

The first step then, is to recruit disciples. These early adopters are the most loyal and productive fans. You'll have to recruit them one at a time and the process will feel agonizing. However, these guys and gals will be those that always respond to emails and surveys.

You'll be able to get honest feedback and consistent commenting from them.

When you see these readers show up, give them the VIP treatment. Respond to every comment, email, and Tweet that they send your way. Help them feel included, like they are part of your process. They will not only appreciate this, but it will build their brand loyalty. Over time, they'll bring more people your way. These people will be vetted already – it's kind of like referring someone for a job. So, they are risking their reputation on this, as small as it might be.

Treat their friends like VIP's as well. 25% of them might stick around, and bring a few more people your way, but if you keep this process up, you'll see the efforts of your engagement start to multiply.

Once you've recruited your disciples, teach them how to reach out to more people. Consider giving them review copies of your products so that they can write a review for you. If you don't have anything to sell, ask them to recommend you on LinkedIn or on another blog. It's this process, word of mouth, that will help you grow like wildfire.

To recruit disciples, try reaching out to other blogging communities. One powerful method is to subscribe to 10-15 relevant blogs in your niche, by email, and try to comment early and often on any new posts that come in. Make sure the comments are useful ("great post!" doesn't work), and then stick around to watch the other commenters trickle in.

Respond to those commenters, even if they don't respond to you. Engage the people in these communities so that they remember your name.

They will eventually recognize your Gravatar and consider you a valuable part of that community. When this happens, many of them will come to visit your blog as another place to hang out.

Again, if you are engaging these communities, you should recognize their name. Give them the VIP treatment as well.

Create a "Lived In" Effect

If your blog is young, and you are having difficulty keeping people around, consider creating or joining a blog network. Although most A-Listers won't reveal this, most of them are part of a network, either publicly or privately.

Essentially, a blog network is a partnership in which you agree to help promote each other's blogs in exchange for them promoting yours. It could even extend to mediums like Twitter, Digg, Facebook, and StumbleUpon.

These networks are effective because you can comment on each other's blogs so that it doesn't look like there aren't any visitors. When a new reader comes along and sees your blog with several comments, there is a certain amount of built in social proof that will encourage them to follow suit and either leave a comment or subscribe.

The same process works for RSS counts. If a reader sees a blog with several thousand subscribers, they are much more likely to tag along than they would be if a blog only shows a few hundred subscribers. Therefore, I wouldn't recommend displaying your count publicly until it reaches 1,000 subscribers.

Give It All Away

Not a single blogger featured here began their career by monetizing immediately. Brian Clark gave content away on **Copyblogger** for years before he tried to monetize. The same is true of Gary Vaynerchuk, who recorded a new show every single day for years before **Wine Library** took off.

As we mentioned in previous chapters, guys like Jonathan Fields and Chris Guillebeau created audiences overnight by giving away great free books, each of which contained some of their most interesting and inspiring content.

Building trust and authority takes time, and it isn't something that you can do easily unless you are willing to put in the work. You don't have to post every single day, but sticking to an editorial schedule will help your audience know what to expect.

Although some bloggers might recommend that you avoid early monetization, the truth is that many of the bloggers featured here monetized early and often…with much success.

Thanks to Jonathan **Field's Firefly Manifesto**, he was able to sell more books, even though he wasn't that well known at the time. Shama Hyder sold B2B consulting, David Risley sold memberships and advertising, while John Chow made no bones about his desire to market everything under the sun. Conversely, Chris Brogan often jokes that he waited 11 years before he asked anything of his audience. However, his blog isn't necessarily built to sell as much as it is built to function as a resume to attract businesses to hire him.

Which means that your blogging audience might not represent the audience that you monetize to. For instance, Shama Kabani blogs to users, but sells to businesses. Shama.

TV functions as a billboard for her knowledge and expertise. iJustine doesn't sell a thing to her YouTube viewers, instead she relies on advertisers to pay her way.

So, it seems that the trick really isn't when to monetize, but how and where to monetize. Don't assume that you have to monetize directly to your readers. As long as you are giving away content, you will be continuously building a bigger audience, which means that your monetization options will increase.

Consider giving away the why, and selling the how. During our interviews, several of the bloggers joked that although you might give away 99% of your best content, you'd be amazed by the number of people that would be willing to pay a high price for the remaining 1%.

It's called content marketing, and it is a highly effective way to build that tribe around your brand. In essence, you are giving people a chance to try before they buy. You are proving yourself to them so that they feel comfortable enough to buy from you. This is how you build repeat business, and highly devoted fans.

In closing, I'll summarize what Chris Guillebeau writes on his blog's about page:

> *All of the essays on this blog and in my newsletter are free, and I won't force you to pay for content. However, if you support me and want to learn more, here are a few books you might find useful.*

Notice the lack of a hard sell? It works for him to the tune of $5k/month.

Selling advertising on blogs

Many bloggers, including some of our featured bloggers chose initially to go down the Adsense route with pay per click advertising. Most moved away from it, as they felt the ads being served weren't always representative of the content and may not be for products they would happily endorse.

Almost all of them do offer advertising on their websites - slots for small banner ads that are usually paid for with a simple monthly fee. There are a whole host of companies who can serve ads on behalf of a network, but the drawback is that they are often not interested until a blog's traffic is significant, at which point most bloggers find it relatively easy to sell the advert spaces themselves and pocket all of the income from an advertiser, instead of a percentage!

The secret seems to be to offer advertising spaces on your blog as early as you can full some spaces, then to experiment with pricing, bearing in mind that there is only so much real estate you can sell on a blog. As traffic grows, renegotiate for better terms.

The convention in blogging seems to have moved away from banner ads, to 125 by 125 pixel ads, with 6 or 8 on the sidebar. This can provide a steady, stable income for a blogger, and any empty space can be filled with affiliate offers.

Having something to sell

This book is about blogging, but it's also about making money. There are millions of bloggers in the world who don't earn money either directly or indirectly through their blogs, but ultimately, most have a goal of generating some income from their work.

We have seen from the examples in this book that there is some quite serious money to be made. Every single blogger featured is earning more than six figure incomes, and I suspect a few are well into seven figures.

We've seen a contrast here once again – Penelope uses her blog to generate business for her company, David sells membership products on his site, most offer some affiliated products, and a few have used their blogs as a platform for launching a career as an author.

Let's look at each of the categories and see what we can learn. At the end of the day, we need something to sell on or via our blogs to actually earn an income:

A Physical Business

A conventional business can be superbly promoted via a blog. Any kind of blog can create a community and a buzz, and it can also greatly increase the "net" of prospects captured by a business.

Let me give you an example. Let's imagine a realtor in London, who has a website that is very well optimized, as you'd expect. Anyone Googling "Apartments to rent in London" will likely find them. But here's the problem – they're often capturing their leads very late in the process, or after the leads have started to talking to other agents.

So let's create a blog for the realtor. And let's not talk about property at all on it. Make it a general blog about London. There can be a section on baby clothes stores, schools, areas, parks - anything you like. Now you're capturing leads from people in the first stages of considering a move. Maybe they are about to have a baby and need a bigger apartment. Perhaps they want to explore other areas of the metropolis, or find out about places where they can roller skate or horse ride. They are likely to do all these things before narrowing down to look at specific apartments for rent. The blog has not only greatly increased the "net" of leads, but it has also given our realtor a chance to help and to generate a sense of community, thus making it far more likely that people will do business with them.

Penelope Trunk, Chris Brogan and Gary Vaynerchuk have all used their blogs to drive business to conventional companies in exactly this way, with some spectacular results.

Digital Products

This is where most bloggers succeed at earning a good income. Selling digital products has been a great source of revenue since the days when bloggers would burn CDs of information and post them to their clients, as David Risley did with his first E-Books.

They have evolved along with the Internet, and pretty much anything is now available for instant download, from simple E-Books, to sophisticated video and audio training courses, with prices varying from a couple of dollars to several thousand.

And around blogging a whole industry has sprung up providing themes, graphics and designs to allow bloggers to create ever more sophisticated websites and pages to sell their products from.

The beauty of offering digital products is that there are no real costs associated with their storage and delivery, so it can be an extremely profitable part of a blogger's business. Darren Rowse recently launched a first E-Book on his Digital Photography School site and grossed $72,000 in a week!

The only costs coming from this would have been his time to create the book, some contribution towards bandwidth, and the small percentage charged to accept credit cards.

For many of the top bloggers, the humble E-Book has evolved into longer term membership programs Lasting from 3 to 6 months, these are often supported by private forums, webinars and coaching calls.

These membership programs are very much in vogue at the moment, and there are several really high powered programs on the market, which provide a great deal of learning, and often access to the material for life, once the initial program has been completed.

Consulting

Many bloggers choose to go down the consultancy route once they have established themselves and their credibility. Simply being a successful blogger qualifies them, to some extent, to offer their services to business and individuals needing help and advice about social media.

The biggest problem with offering a consultancy service is that you are effectively back to trading your time for money, and therefore you aren't really leveraging the power of the Internet to attract large numbers. It can be an effective income earner, as long as you can charge an appropriately high rate for your time.

Of the people featured in *Beyond Blogging*, Chris Garrett seems to be doing the most consultancy work, and it's no surprise because he earned his first online income by going down that route.

Several of our bloggers are also accomplished public speakers, and they often address large audiences, either from private companies or at trade conventions. Some of these gigs will be well-paid, although often only travel and expenses are covered.

Books

It once seemed that getting a book deal was the Holy Grail for bloggers. Although many still harbor a secret desire to be published as a conventional author, it's no longer seen in the same way.

Having said that, a blog is simply an amazing platform from which to launch a book, and both Gary Vaynerchuk and Chris Brogan have used their blogs to launch best-sellers. A blog with a hundred thousand regular readers almost guarantees a flying start to sales for any book. Interestingly, the publishing industry has finally become aware of this and are now actively encouraging their existing authors to become active in social media.

If your objective is to become a print author, then blogging is a perfect way to kick-start that career, and at the same time, if you are successful in creating a very widely read blog, you'll find the book deals coming to you anyway. Gary proved this by landing a 10 book, seven-figure deal on the strength of his video blogging!

At the very least, posting to a blog every day will hone your writing skills and polish up your prose! So, it's fascinating that blogs have now come full circle, from the antithesis of conventional print, to the best way to promote and launch any conventional print product.

Summary

We've examined the different types of product that bloggers sell, and how they make their money from doing so. Deciding what's right for your blog should be based on what's right for your readers, and you can find this out by talking with them and by conducting surveys. But the key message is that blogs are both a great platform to generate direct sales, and at the same time a terrific place to promote an existing product or business.

All of our featured bloggers use a combination of all of the above to drive their considerable incomes, and that seems to be a recipe for sustained success.

Expanding Your Game

Being a six figure blogger is great, but in our opinion, blogging should be treated as a means to an end, rather than the end itself. For instance, it's hard to tell how long blogging will be a popular medium to consume content. What happens if people stop reading blogs and your income depends on them doing so? Your business is over…right?

So, consider using blogging as a stepping stone, so that you can become more than just a blogger. Don't view blogging as the endgame, but instead as just a part of the business building process.

As an example, we'll consider the work of Jonathan Fields, who built a blog solely for selling a book. He builds businesses, not blogs. The blog was simply a tool to help him create more opportunity.

David Risley sells information, but not so much as a blogger but as a technology expert. Should blogs fold, he could sell a newsletter, a magazine, or a DVD.

Penelope Trunk is a published author, is frequently found on television, and writes for major news publications.

Although her blog pays her well, it serves primarily as a PR tool.

Gary Vaynerchuk isn't just a wine blogger, as he runs a massive consulting business, has a seven-figure book deal, and runs a multi-million dollar wine franchise.

Both *Wine Library* and *GaryVaynerchuk.com* serve as promotional tools for his personal brand, not as primary revenue streams.

At the risk of sounding like a broken record, I'll stop there, but I think you get the idea. Creating an online business is exactly that…a business.

Treat it like one

Treat your blog like a business. Realize that in order to run a successful business, you'll need to eventually hand the reigns over to someone else, either to an employee or via the sale of your business. As your empire expands, and your opportunities increase, you will reach a point in which your very presence is holding you back from progress. In other words, don't try to do everything yourself.

One of the commonalities between the bloggers listed here is that they all recruit and develop talent. Chris Guillebeau hired rockstar designer Reese Spykerman before he started making a lot of money. However, it was this very act that gave his business that image of non-conformity.

Gary Vaynerchuk has an incredible staff of helpers that guide him from task to task. He can't do all the filming, designing, editing, and writing on his own. That's not his talent – his is building businesses.

Darren Rowse has an awesome personal assistant and program manager that works behind the scenes to make sure that all of his sites run smoothly and without the need for his direct involvement. This frees him to work on bigger things.

Brian Clark works with the wonderfully talented Sonia Simone, a fantastic blogger in her own right. She's the chief editor at **Copyblogger** and works very closely with him on **Teaching Sells** in order to keep the customers happy and let him manage the business.

Again, I don't want to beat a dead horse any more than I already have, but the recurring theme is that you need to recruit and develop talent so that you can become greater than you already are. Take a look at any millionaire, hell, any six figure earner, and you'll find a silent partner that works in the background to help things run efficiently. That's the type of person you will need to find.

Recruit designers, content authors, ghost writers, copy writers, developers, and anyone else you need to in order to create the best product that you can. Work with a VA when you can afford one, so that you can see the big picture.

If you get tied up in the little things, you'll never be able to expand your game.

Define the Next Level

In order to take your game to the next level, you'll need to define what that next level looks like. Is it a book deal, a movie, or a consulting firm? Do you want to run a blog network?

Maybe you want to get a TV gig on the Food Network or on the Discovery Channel. The options are only as limited as you force them to be. Your vision will guide the future of your business, but you'll need to establish it before you get started. Sure, it might change, but at least you'll have a goal…a destination at which to arrive.

Once you define it, create a list of goals to get you there. What does it look like when you do arrive? What does the progression look like? Who will you need to have on your team? Who will you need to create JV deals with?

The answers to these questions will guide you toward that next level, so take care when answering them. The world is yours for the taking, but you will have to step up and claim it.

In the beginning, you'll want to establish an income so that you can invest in future opportunities. How many E-Books do you need to sell in order to meet your income goals? How many more do you need to meet your lifestyle goals?

How many small blogs, earning $100/month each, do you need in order to buy a larger blog? How many memberships do you need to sell before you can hire that rockstar developer to build your dream business for you?

If it's consulting that you do, then look at what Shama Kabani and Jonathan Fields earn per client. They can charge thousands because they earn more than that for their clients. Shama's business reached six figures in its first year, and is poised to become a seven figure business in the near future.

Each of the people in this book are constantly building, evaluating, and improving. They don't stop at one product – they consistently move towards a greater goal. It doesn't have to be monetary, it could be that you travel the world or spend more time at home with your family. Sometimes, it is simply a matter of earning enough to live your perfect day.

Your own paradise is achievable. You can become the superstar that you want to be, but you've got to accept that it can be done. It's going to take some time, and it's going to take some thought, but once you realize that achieving a desired result is nothing more than completing a series of actions, you will become unstoppable. And that's how you become the next guy in this book, or on the cover of your own.

Final Note

This has been a fascinating journey, and we hope you have enjoyed reading about our bloggers as much as we have writing about them. They are an inspiring bunch, and we have no doubt that they are the current cream of the crop.

We hope you have been inspired and that you now realize that by following their lead you can carve out a career for yourself online - either as a blogger or by using a blog as a platform for some other kind of business.

Do you have what it takes to go "***Beyond Blogging***?"

www.ingramcontent.com/pod-product-compliance
Lightning Source LLC
Chambersburg PA
CBHW031840170526
45157CB00001B/366